THE
ONCORHYNCHUS AFFAIR

WILLIAM S LEET

Acknowledgments

The Chinook salmon on the cover was printed by Christopher M. Dewees, a master of gyotaku fish printing. I am grateful for his permission to use it on my cover. My wife, Mary-Helen, very much enjoyed following the development of the story and offered valuable suggestions throughout. Joan Peterson read the manuscript and imparted some very good advice. So did David Robertson. I thank you all.

For my Family

FOREWORD

Life is miraculous. The complex networks in the life cycle of some multi-host parasites defy belief. The life history of Chinook salmon (*Oncorhynchus tshawytscha*) is fascinating because, like other salmon, most return to their natal spawning grounds. Some migrations are nearly 2,000 miles long. Even in less distant migrations, salmon face many perils as they ascend rivers to spawn – far more now than when they evolved during the Triassic period.

CHAPTER ONE

Melting snowflakes sent droplets of water down Jennifer's forehead and into her eyes, as she stuffed her fisted hands into the pockets of the down coat she had plucked from her father's closet. Waiting for the next vehicle, a wave of guilt passed as she wondered about her mother's ability to get along on her own. *She'll do okay. Better than okay, actually.* She took her hands from her pockets and brushed some of the snow from her shoulders and from her wool watch cap, then thrust them back into the pockets of the olive green coat. Fourteen cars and eight trucks had passed her since her mom, in tears, had dropped her at the freeway entrance. Estimating that it had been about an hour ago, she pushed her mitten cuff down to look at her watch. Fifteen minutes. *What in God's name am I doing?*, thought the seventeen-year-old.

She shivered convulsively, automatically showing her thumb to a Kenwood diesel as it approached. The big metallic green rig stopped. At that moment, Jenny didn't know what to do. As she bent to pick up her backpack, she sobbed.

"Fer Christ's sake, get in," she heard as she strove to overcome the fear that inundated her. "Get in. We're stopping traffic. Get in."

Jenny looked up at the big truck wondering how in the world she would ever be able to get into it. The door opened as she stepped up and grabbed onto a vertical chrome handle next to it. With a herculean effort she swung all of her five-feet four-inches and 115-pounds into the seat of the immaculately clean cab. It was warm inside and country music was playing just loud enough to be heard over the engine noise.

"Where ya headed?" the driver called out as he ran through an endless sequence of gears.

"Berkeley, California."

"Well, I ain't goin' there, but I can take you part way. What the hell do you want to go way out there for, anyways?"

"I'm going to graduate school."

"Graduate school." He looked over at her two or three times and finally muttered, "Jesus." That ended the conversation for some ten minutes, during which time Jenny reconsidered the wisdom of this journey she was making. Then, very earnestly, he yelled, "Don't be scared."

That is exactly what she was. "I'm not."

"Well, you should be."

"You just said not to be."

"Well, you should be scared, ridin' with a stranger and all, but you don't need to be 'cause I ain't gonna hurt ya or nothin'. I ain't gonna hurt ya or even turn on the charm. I'll try to be good comp'ny though. M' name's Mike. Mike Simmons. What's yours?"

"Jennifer Lindsey."

"Jennifer Lindsey. Are you the famous Jennifer Lindsey?"

"I didn't even know there was one."

"I don't know if there is one, I just wanted to know if you were famous. I guess not too many famous people are out hitchin' rides, but, you never know."

"I didn't expect you to stop this big rig. Do you pick up people often?"

"Nope. Never did it before. Do you hitch hike often?"

"Nope. This is the first time. We're both first-timers, I

guess." *I hope we don't have to keep up some stupid conversation very long,* Jenny thought.

"We'll be havin' lunch in Erie," Then Mike added with a sense of pride, "I'll buy."

"You don't need to do that. I've got money."

"How much you got?"

"Well, if you really must know, I've got about two hundred dollars."

"Okay, Jennifer Lindsey, you failed the first test. I sure as hell don't need to know how much you got, and neither does anybody else. "I'm buying. Meanwhile, don't tell anybody you're packin' two c-notes. That's a lota money." There was a tone of finality in everything Mike said, as if his was the last word.

Suddenly, overtaken by fatigue, Jenny fell into a deep sleep. She was aware of the motion and the engine noise of the big eighteen wheeler, but she was in such a deep sleep that she felt almost paralyzed. When Mike pulled into a parking lot four hours later, she saw that they were at Johnny's Cafe near Erie. "We're eatin' here. I've been here before. It's not too bad," Mike said, as he shuffled all around his truck checking things. He saw Jenny looking at the chrome silhouettes of women – apparently naked – on his mud-flaps and remarked, "Hey, I said not to worry." They ordered hamburgers. "Well, how do you like ridin' in a truck?" His voice was still loud and had a hollow tone.

"Fine. Actually, I don't know. You probably noticed I was passed out most of the way. I think my emotions caught up with me. I did enjoy the ride, though. Thanks for picking me up. You surprised me. I never expected a truck to stop." Mike had a look of amusement as they sat looking at each other, Jenny feeling a little out of place.

She was looking at his eyebrows, which were connected in the middle.

"Like that mono-brow?" he asked with a muffled giggle. Then he laughed out loud. "I used to have a girlfriend who made me pluck it. Jesus Christ, what a deal." In a loud voice he added, "It *hurt* for chrisakes."

Jenny smiled. "You shouldn't have done it. I mean just because a girlfriend told you to? Bum girlfriend, Mike. What's in your truck?"

"You, me, and enough maple syrup for all the pancakes and waffles in Amarillo for a few months, I guess. But first I'm headed home. Home to Wichita. The wife'll have some kind of fancy dinner for me tomorrow night when I get there. I'm drivin' straight through. I'll spend the night and then go on to Amarillo."

"How far is Wichita."

"It's a ways, little girl. I don't count miles. Just hours. Like I said, I'll get there tomorrow night. Let's go. If you're going all the way to Berkeley and you have two-hundred dollars, why the hell are you hitch hiking. You could probably fly out there for less than that."

"Then I'd get there without any money. Two-hundred is all I could scrape together."

Mike considered what Jenny said. It made some sense, but not a lot. Jennifer looked pretty vulnerable. "You don't look much like a seasoned hitch hiker," he said.

"I already told you I've never hitchhiked before. I've never even ridden in a truck before. In fact, I've never even been this far away from home."

"A lot of firsts. Ya didn't pick a very nice day to start out, snowin' and all. What the hell are you doing, anyways, little girl? I thought school started in the fall."

"It's a long story," Jenny said, again flooding with fear and uncertainty.

"Well, it's still a long ways to Wichita."

"Why did you pick me up? To be honest, I'm still scared. Not of you. Just of what I'm doing. I don't even know what's ahead. I'm just heading west. I must be nuts."

"To be honest, I picked you up because you looked a little needy. I think you'll be all right, but if ya want t' go back just say the word. If you want to keep going, let's get the hell out of here, and you can tell me what's on your mind."

They climbed into the cab and when Mike reached cruising speed, Jenny said, "Well, my father shot himself, and a week later, Father Mark, the parish priest, tried to get into my shorts."

"That's a pretty eventful week."

"As soon as it became clear what he had in mind, I pretended like I was going to cooperate and instead did something that will probably cause him to smart a little whenever he takes a whiz. You know, not forever, but for a couple weeks, I expect. I talked to the Monsignor about it and that coward said he'd 'look into it. He never will."

"Jesus, now I'm scared," Mike quipped. "Seriously, you've had some bad shit come yer way. Now I don't want to pop yer bubble or discourage you, but running away may not be yer best answer, hear what I'm sayin'?"

"I know. I do know that. But it wasn't like that. I've been planning this trip for a year. This stuff just happened to happen right before I was going to leave. My dad was crazy but nobody knew it but Mom and me. He was on the faculty at SUNY, that's the university in Albany, and somehow they found out he had had a sex for grades system going on for several years. I'm not going to go into the details, but he was a very smart man who made life miserable for others in order to make it gratifying to himself. I don't know. He was nuts, but also a schemer. I usually just tell people that he was crazy, but there was a little more to it than that. My family should have been a case study for a dysfunctionality workshop. He really started coming apart this last year."

"In all the years I've been driving a truck, I've never picked up a hitchhiker, and when I do, it turns out to be a real case. I mean you're a case! You don't even look old enough to be out of high school."

"Well, I graduated from high school – early, in fact, but I'm not really going to graduate school. I haven't even been to college yet, but I'm on my way. That's why I'm headed for Berkeley. I've got this backpack with a prepaid cell phone that my mom bought for me, some of my clothes, the money I told you about, and a fake I.D. that says I'm Amy Toth, age 22. There's even a pistol in there. I figured my dad wouldn't need it any more now that he's finished blowing his brains out."

"Yer not serious."

"Serious."

"Jenny you've got to wise up. One, yer stupid to be carrying a gun around. If you're going to do that, I sure as hell wouldn't be telling anyone about it. Same as the money deal. Fer chrisakes, keep a lid on it."

"I know. Even though I'm only seventeen, I'm pretty good at figuring out who I can trust."

"Get rid of the damn pistol. You don't need it, and it'll get you in trouble. If you keep it, don't mention it again – even to someone you trust. Hear me?"

"Okay. Okay. I thought you'd laugh the way I said it. My dad really is better off dead. But he was my dad, even if he knocked me around a little bit."

"Well, Jenny, maybe yer doin' the right thing. Maybe not. But if you put a couple miles between you and the crazies, by and by maybe you'll forget about 'em. I hope so, anyways."

Jenny began to feel at home with Mike and continued to tell some of the bizarre stories that comprised her youth. As daylight began to evaporate, they got to Elkhart, Indiana and stopped for dinner at Denny's. "I lived in Oregon for years," Mike offered. "Probably go back there eventually." He disposed of a beer in about thirty seconds, and they each gobbled up a Salisbury steak.

"What did you do there? Drive a truck?"

"Nope. I worked for my dad. He has a fishing boat – a troller – out in Coos Bay. That's a fishing port in southern Oregon. My dad's a commercial fisherman – mostly salmon, but if the run's not on, he'll find something else – crabs in the winter – sometimes rockfish. Salmon fishin' ain't what it used to be because for years they've been making life tough for salmon. Have you ever heard of the Grand Coulee Dam?"

"Nope."

"Well, it's a dam on the Columbia, and salmon can't get by it. There's no ladder or nothin'. There used to be hundreds of miles of salmon spawning riffles upstream of that dam. The fish that spawned up there were huge – 80 pounds or more, I think. Dad called 'em hogs. *His* dad –

he was also a salmon fisherman – used to talk about how sad it was that there were no more hogs. The dam was built way before even my dad was born, so I never saw one and neither did he. I saw some big Chinooks, but no hogs. Now, I think there's something like 10 dams on the Columbia before you even get to the Grand Coulee. They have fish ladders so the salmon can go upstream, but the spawning riffles are gone."

"What do you mean by spawning riffles?"

"That's where salmon spawn – in the riffles in rivers where the water flows swiftly over gravel and rocks. They call em spawning riffles."

"I didn't know that. I thought salmon were in the ocean."

"They are. They swim upstream to spawn. That's where they're born. Then they grow for awhile in the stream but after a year or two – it depends on the kind of salmon – they get a huge urge to swim out to sea. It means they have to change somehow, I can't explain it, but to go from freshwater to saltwater stresses em. They breathe through their gills and when they go into saltwater their gills, hell, their whole body has to change. Then they go back to fresh water. My dad used to get pretty excited when he'd explain it to me. The big miracle is that when they're ready to spawn, they almost always go back to the same river and the same place in the river where they were born. Then they die."

"I wonder how they know where they came from – I mean what river."

"That's the miraculous part. They can smell the water where they spend the first year of their life. Smell it! Can you believe it? Not only do they smell it, they remember it's the right smell from the day they begin their down-stream migration. This is after swimming around in the ocean for three or four years. Jesus! Do you suppose you could find your way back to wherever you were born by what it smelled like? Don't even try to answer that, be-cause the answer is hell no."

"I'm surprised you didn't take over your dad's boat and become a commercial fisherman yourself.."

"Take it over? I couldn't take it over cause my dad's still using it. He ain't dead like yours. He never had occasion to blow his brains out, even though fishin' isn't always good. Nope, he's alive and well. No bullet holes in that dude."

"Well that's true of most people," Jenny replied, again trying to sound a little tougher than she felt.

In the nearly two days they had been together, Jenny felt she knew Mike better than she had ever known her own father. She knew there must be a lot to know about this man, but they were getting close to Ames, Iowa, which Mike had already told Jenny would be a good place for her to look for another ride. "We'll get a bite to eat here, and I'll show you a map," he said.

"What's your wife's name?" Jenny asked after they sat down in a booth near the door.

"I just call her Sis, and don't ask why. She ain't my sis-ter, if yer thinkin' that."

"Nope. I didn't even try to figure out why. But I won't ask. It will be good to have it be a little mystery."

While they ate, Mike showed Jenny a worn and torn map of the eastern United States. "From here I head south. It won't do you much good to go down to Wichita, so this is where we're going to part ways, unless you want to go out of your way to meet Sis." He looked into her eyes for a clue to what she might be thinking. "Don't you worry, little girl, just pay attention to what people say and do. Be alert, and you'll be okay. Pay attention. That's the main thing."

Jenny felt Mike's kindness. His guidance was real, and he was interesting. Was it too much to hope that she would be so lucky on her next ride? But she had studied his map and agreed with Mike that the road to Wichita would net very little progress westward. Besides she was getting road weary and had figured out a plan for a free night's lodging and shower in the college town. One of her friends was a sorority girl at SUNY so Jenny knew a little about the Greek system.

She walked out to the big Kenworth with Mike, wishing that he was going all the way to Berkeley. Trying her best not to show her despair that she was about to be alone again, she said, "See ya, Mike. Thanks a million. Maybe we can go salmon fishing sometime."

So far, so good, Jenny thought. *Still quite a ways to go, though.*

CHAPTER TWO

Jenny gave Mike a hug before he climbed back into his diesel rig. It was clear and cool, and thankfully, not snowing. She watched him disappear down the freeway, brushed some imaginary snow from her jeans and sweatshirt, slipped into her down jacket, and walked back to the Denny's where they had just eaten. She found *Sororities* in the yellow pages of a phone book she borrowed at the front register and phoned the first one listed. Her call was answered on the second ring, and she told a woman who identified herself as Kathy, that she was Jennifer Lindsey, an A D Pi sister from Syracuse, and she wondered if she could spend the night. After Kathy gave her a warm, enthusiastic invitation, Jenny asked, "How do I get there?"

"No problem, I'll just drive over and pick you up. Where are you calling from?"

Kathy, a pretty girl with rich brown hair and lively blue eyes, got to Denny's in a matter of minutes. She arrived in a yellow Corvette, which somehow seemed out of place in Ames. They made it back to the house before Jenny could ask about the car, or even comment on it. It was well before dinnertime when they arrived giving Jenny time to take a shower.

Kathy and Jenny then joined about fifty other women for lamb chops, mashed potatoes, and peas. The women, sitting six to a table, were served their dinners by young men – probably students. The clinking of glassware and institutional china punctuated the murmur of feminine voices. The rich, garlicky lamb chops filled the room with a smell that reminded Jenny of the anniversary dinner that she had helped her mother prepare for her father the night before he shot himself. Weird. In spite of the grim memory, it smelled delicious.

"God, Jenny, it's so awesome that you're hitching to California," Kathy said as their plates arrived. "Doing something like that would never even occur to me – if it did, I'd be scared to try it. Although if you judged from my car that I might be spoiled, you'd be right. My dad tends to dote on me more than a little bit. I'm going to have to introduce you. It's part of the protocol or etiquette of the sorority house." The girls recited a short grace in unison, and Kathy stood, rang her glass a couple of times with a spoon, and announced, "This is Jennifer Lindsey, from... what chapter is it?"

"Um... Epsilon." Jenny pulled a Greek letter out of her vague memory of the Greek alphabet.

"From the Epsilon chapter at Syracuse University. She's hitchhiking to California... "Aside again, "What is it you're going for?"

"Graduate school at Berkeley."

"She's going to be attending graduate school at Berkeley." The diners applauded politely and Kathy sat down.

The topic of conversation at the table was *Winter Snowflakes*, apparently an annual dance formal at the sorority. Jenny noticed that the conversational style of the girls was different than what she was used to. There was a chirping quality about it. Kathy didn't fit the mold, and Jenny was glad that it had been she who picked her up. The most vociferous chirper was an overweight girl named Beth, who stopped the conversation to let Jenny know that she was not dressed appropriately for dinner, and that hitchhiking was not only dangerous, but not lady-like. Beth's facial skin was milky white with a network of doily-like blue veins faintly visible. Jenny bit her lower lip to keep from saying anything. Apparently fully aware of Jenny's thought process, Kathy shifted the conversation away from the formal dance that was the subject of chirp.

"I play on the Iowa State softball team. We made it to the College World Series playoffs," she said softly to Jenny.

Jenny, happy about the change of subject said, "I love softball. Maybe we could get up a game... or get *in* a game somewhere."

"Not in January, unless you want to freeze to death. But there's some batting cages on the other side of town where you can hit baseballs pitched by a machine. It's fun. If you want to do it, I'll drive if you pay."

"Cool. How much is it?"

"Not much. Five should cover it."

Beth chirped, "It's dangerous over there Kathy. Remember that incident?"

Diplomatically, Kathy said, "That's a good bit of advice. Maybe we won't go there." It turned out to be a fortunate response.

After dinner, Kathy and Jenny excused themselves and went to Kathy's room to set up a place for Jenny to sleep.

"I'm amazed you caught on to Beth so quick," Kathy whispered as they left the dining room. "Her mother was president of the house back in the day so... well, anyhow, that kind of helped her get into the house. Now she thinks she runs it."

"How could you tell that I thought she was a twerp? I tried to be respectful."

"I'm a mind reader."

"It looks to me like Beth needs a few more prunes in her diet. Or maybe a brain transplant. Are you serious about going to the batting cages? If you are, I'm stoked."

"Hell yes. They'll offer us a bat when we get there, but I'll take my Louisville Slugger. The ones they hand out are metal. We'll use mine instead."

"God, your car is beautiful," Jenny said when they got to the yellow 'vette.

"People leave notes on it all the time wanting to know if I'll sell it. Dad gave it to me as a high school graduation present."

"Well you've got a better dad than I did. You really are a peach to take me out to this place. I'm sure you have better things to do on a Friday night."

"Hey, I love to do this. Sometimes I can get a date to go to the cages with me, but the girls in the house have zero interest, and with the guys it's always a one-time deal because I can hit better than they can. Also, there was an incident out there and for awhile they discouraged girls from going ."

"What do you mean by an incident?"

"I'm not really sure. A girl got attacked or something. Anyway, we're almost there."

"I'd better focus my batting eye. It's been awhile since I last swung a bat."

Cornfield Cages was in a retail-industrial complex, but the prevalent smell was still a mix of well-fed cows and new-mown hay. Kathy waited outside the office while Jenny filled in Amy Toth as her name, showed her Georgia I.D., and paid five dollars for fifty pitches. They took turns taking five consecutive swings apiece, and Kathy demonstrated why she was on a championship softball team.

After they had swung at fifty pitches, they stood outside the cage discussing whether to pay for fifty more swings. "I'm good for five more bucks if you want to, Kath. This is fun."

In the distance they saw a tall, thin man in a brimmed hat approaching them through the dim light. "Closin' time, ladies," he said in an exaggerated high-pitched farmer twang.

"Guess that answers our question," said Kathy. The guy kept walking toward them with his right hand in his pocket. It was not the same man that had been in the office when Jenny paid. Both women turned away from him and started back toward the car.

"Now you two little bitches shut up and do exactly what I tell you and we'll all live happily ever after." The guy held a hunting knife to Kathy's neck. "Get rid of that bat, or your sister's dead," he said quietly to Jenny.

Jenny turned loose of the bat and held her hands out to the side in a submissive gesture. After a few seconds passed, she said in a seductive voice, "I love sex." She dropped her coat on the ground and quickly slipped out of her sweatshirt.

"Come on, Cowboy. Let's get it on. I love it."

The guy's jaw dropped almost as fast as the knife, which clattered harmlessly on the concrete walkway. As he stared at Jenny's youthful breasts, Kathy scrambled out of his grasp, and Jenny quickly picked up the Louisville Slugger and swung it at his head as hard as she could. She connected.

"God," Kathy gasped. "We better call the cops." She put her hands to her face in revulsion, as the guy lay motionless on the concrete.

"Let's go. We'll call 'em from the sorority." Jenny grabbed her coat and struggled into her sweatshirt as they hustled back to the car. After the car was started and they had driven about a block, Jenny said, "We're not calling the cops."

"What do you mean? I'm scared."

"So am I. Can you keep a secret?"

"I guess so, why?"

"Because we've got a big one, Kathy."

"What do you mean?"

"What I mean is that we aren't going to tell anybody that we had anything to do with that creep getting a lump on his head."

"The guy saw us. You're gone – outta here; but Ames isn't exactly a huge city. He's liable to find me, and... God help me."

"Kathy... listen. I'm pretty sure I didn't kill him. Although head injuries can be a little misleading. But the really good part is that el creepo won't remember anything that happened for a minute or so before I hit him. A doctor told me that once. It's a type of amnesia. That guy lying back there on the ground isn't the same guy who was in the office. He was just some random maniac. Let's go someplace and get some ice cream or something. I'm shaking like a leaf. We have to calm down before we go back to your sorority."

"God, I just want to get back."

"It's better to unwind first. If we're hysterical or in shock we won't be able to keep the secret. Right now, that is life's most important mission."

"How can you be sure what's the right thing to do. Jeez, I'm only a year behind you in school, and it seems like you're ten times as smart as I am."

"I've gone through some weird stuff – some stuff that kind of forced a steep learning curve on me in certain situations."

"Jenny... the cops are going to get involved in our little adventure whether that hayseed lives or dies."

"You may be right, Kathy. You probably are. But if we lay low, we won't get hassled. They won't know we participated."

Back in the campus area, Kathy parked in front of a soda fountain. The two girls entered and sat down at a white, looped wire table along the back wall. Each ordered a hot fudge sundae, and while they were waiting, Jenny said, "I used to work in a place like this. In fact, I just quit a week ago."

"In Syracuse?"

"No. In Albany. I didn't go to Syracuse, and I'm not really an A D Pi. I just graduated from high school. I was planning to tell you before we went to sleep, but the evening didn't exactly unfold as expected. Somehow it seemed to me safer to be a twenty-two year old hitchhiker going to grad school than a seventeen-year-old one."

"Jeez, Jenny, I *can not* believe it. I just wish you were going to be around for awhile. You know, so we could give each other a little moral support."

"We'll be okay, Kathy. Friends for life. We can keep in touch by texting or email, no problem. You're going to have to let me know if the corn picker wakes up."

"Can you at least stay for a couple of days?"

"Well, I feel like I want to get there. I really *am* going to the University of California. I've been accepted for the spring semester, and it starts in three weeks, so I have to make tracks."

"How about staying one more day. Maybe my dad can help you."

"How do you think he could help?"

"He's got a plane."

"Come on. Your dad's not going to fly me out there."

"He just might. He would for sure if I tell him you saved my life. Do you think I should tell him?"

"Hmm. Let's think about that one for awhile. We definitely don't want to do it to buy a ride. If he'll give me a ride that's great, but we don't want to bribe him. This evening really has to be a secret from everyone."

"Why don't you gamble a day on the come?"

"What the hell does that mean?"

"I can't believe I said something that you don't understand. I thought you knew everything."

"Hardly. What's it mean?"

"It just means it will cost you one day in your schedule, but you might come out a winner if my dad decides to fly you out there – even part way."

"What a cool way to say it."

"Do you think of yourself as a high ball hitter?"

"What do you mean?"

"Well, you were having some trouble with pitches in the strike zone, but you got all of that guy's head. It was a good foot and a half above the top of the strike zone."

"Maybe it helped that his head was bigger than a baseball."

"You've got a point, Jenny. The scouting report on you would say, 'goes deep on the high, hard one.' Or maybe, 'Hits well in the clutch.'"

"Maybe it would just say, 'Hits the head well.' If nothing else, it would confuse the reader."

"'Hits best without shirt.'"

"What a riot! So, what's your last name, anyway, Kathy?"

"Belton. Is yours truly Lindsey; or is that just another one of your safety net ideas?"

"Yep, Lindsey it is."

"Tomorrow I'll take you out to our farm. You'll like my dad. He's a good one."

CHAPTER THREE

The next day they combed through the newspaper and found no mention of any altercation at the Cornfield Cages. "I think that's probably good news," Jenny said.

"I hope you're right," responded a still-shaken Kathy Belton, as she drove Jenny over to her dad's farm.

The Belton place was huge, with undulating waves of plowed soil rolling to the horizon. In the cleared area adjacent to the road were silos, barns, machine shops, and equipment buildings. Kathy explained that each building served a specific need in the functioning of the farm. To one side of the maintenance area was a large landscaped yard with a pond surrounded by two or more acres of lawn. There, a pair of mallards lazed in the slanting sun rays. The house was an immaculate two story colonial style, newly painted – probably not more than twenty years old. A retriever came running out of the yard, barking and jumping in circles and wiggling all over. It was clearly pleased to see Kathy and spent a few moments of dog curiosity with Jenny. They found Mr. Belton in one of the machine shops. "Hi, Dad. This is my new friend Jennifer Lindsey. She goes by Jenny."

"Hello, Jenny." John Belton was tall and handsome. There are very few men that Jenny would describe as handsome on the first cut, but in Mr. Belton's case there was no other way. Six-two or -three, dark wavy hair, dark eyebrows, and deep blue eyes. It seemed a trite way to think about it, but he belonged on the screen. He held out his hand, took Jenny's, and clasped his other over the top of it. "I'm happy to meet you. Are you a student here at Iowa State?"

"She's an A D Pi from Syracuse. She played softball there, and when we played Syracuse in the playoffs, Jenny was the shortstop. I didn't meet her then, but she came to visit the house yesterday on her way to California."

"Well, I'm sorry your friendship is to be so short-lived. When do you leave?"

"Tomorrow."

"Dad, do you have any business west of here any time soon?"

"Yes, I do. I have to be in Salt Lake City on Monday. I'm planning to leave tomorrow and spend Sunday night in one of the downtown hotels."

"Are you taking your plane?"

"Yes. Want to go along?"

"We do. Yippee! You won on the come, Jenny."

Mr. Belton said, "I'll be delighted to have the company of two such lovely ladies."

Later Jenny asked Kathy if she routinely laid b.s. on her dad the way she had with the bogus softball playoff story.

"Not ever. Not with anybody, in fact. I just thought it would be fun to try it. No harm, no foul. I wouldn't ever do anything that would reduce the high esteem my dad holds for me. He's a super guy, and I want to stay on his good side. In fact you and my dad have something in common."

"What?"

"You have each saved my life one time."

"Wow, what happened?"

"Long story. But true. I'll tell you some day. Maybe."

For the remainder of the day, it was all they could do to stay away from the scene of the crime. They were dying to find out anything they could about the Cornfield Cages rapist, as they named him, but prudence prevailed and Kathy gave

Jenny a guided tour of Ames. That night they decided that taking in a movie would be safe and sane.

Early the following morning after packing a few extras to take along on the trip, they went out to the airport, prepped Mr. Belton's twin engine Cessna for take off, and headed west. Except for one moment of terror, the trip to California was going way better than Jenny could ever have hoped. Now she was on her first plane ride, and it was going to deposit her a day or two from her destination, depending on... well, the variables were too numerous for her to contemplate, but she was thankful for the good fortune that had cradled her trip so far. Meanwhile, they were cruising at 200 knots – four and half-hours of travel time to Salt Lake City compared to around twenty if they had been driving, and who knows how many hitchhiking? A few puffy clouds dotted the sky out to the horizon, and the face of America was laid out below in vast geometric patterns.

"How did you know how to find the airport?" Jenny asked as they began their descent.

"Luck," was the deadpan reply.

They registered at the Salt Lake City Hotel – one room for Mr. Belton and one for Kathy and Jenny. Jenny put on some fancy clothes that Kathy loaned her. When she looked in the mirror she saw a young woman of grace and beauty, and for a moment Jenny wondered about her usual style of dressing, which had become part of her persona. Maybe I owe myself something a little bit better, she decided.

Mr. Belton took them to dinner at an elegant restaurant that wouldn't serve the Bordeaux wine that they had brought because it was Sunday evening. But they ate fancy food served by men who performed as if they were being filmed. Jenny didn't care about the wine, because she was still floating on air from the flight. The Dom Perignon that they drank in Mr. Belton's room probably contributed.

Jenny was charmed by Mr. Belton ("call me Belt"). He was genteel but humorous. After they had been eating for awhile, Jenny told him that she would be starting college as a freshman at the University of California – that the Syracuse story was one they had made up just for fun. She felt like a fool telling him but wanted Belt to have the truth. She was beginning to believe that even though half a nation would separate them, she had found life-long friends. She learned that Belt was a widower and that he and Kathy and a younger brother had moved to Ames after the death of his wife. Kathy mentioned that he was seeing a lot of a professor at the University. "She's going to be trouble if my dad doesn't dump her," she told Jenny later.

Jenny and Kathy stayed up late that night talking in their room. "I'm still fretting over your big hit at the cages, Jenny. Are you sure I'm not doomed to receive some kind of retaliation?"

"There are a couple of very fortunate things that happened that night Kathy. One is that *I* paid and signed us in. Another is that you waited outside. Another is that you wore your baseball hat with your hair tucked up. But the luckiest is that I used a fake name and fake street in a real city. There's no way el creepo will have any clue about who either one of us is. Anyway, the amnesia deal is a for sure. It's a medical fact. The one unfortunate thing is that you probably have the only yellow Corvette in Ames. Hopefully nobody came by and saw it parked there."

"How did you give a fake name? I thought you had to show your driver's license to the guy in the office."

Jenny showed her fake I.D. to Kathy and told her that an acquaintance had made it, but that she wasn't sure why he had given it to her. "I know Atlanta is real, but who knows if there's an Estates Drive there? Who knows if there's even a person anywhere named Amy Toth?"

"Amy?"

"Yeah?"

"How come you answered if your name's not Amy?" Kathy had a huge smile, like *am I tricking you or are you tricking me.* "Who the hell are you anyway?. How am I supposed to know that Jenny isn't the bogus name? I like to know who I'm with when I'm involved in clubbings."

"My name really is Jennifer Lindsey. But by putting Amy Toth on the register, I might have prevented us from getting involved in a lot of bothersome inquiry. Remember, Kathy, we just defended ourselves. It's not like we committed a crime."

"You defended me, you mean. Keep in mind, Jen, I was the one with the knife in my throat. That corn picker didn't look like he was too interested in leaving any witnesses behind. I'm pretty sure he was going to rape us one at a time and kill us. Something similar happened there once before. I'm not exactly sure how it went down, but it was some kind of assault on a woman. By the way, how come you're traveling under a false name with false credentials?"

"It was kind of a lark at first. This guy I barely know gave me the license as a going away gift. I started thinking about my situation – you know, a seventeen-year-old girl hitchhiking across the country, and I decided I've got this fake identity; I might just as well use it. Maybe it will offer some measure of protection."

"I think it already did. Very fortuitous that you used it at the cages."

"No doubt. Anyway, as the saying goes, all's well that ends well. Which brings me to something I've been thinking about. Kath – why don't you head on out to Berkeley with me?"

"I'm less than a year away from graduating from Iowa State, Jenny. Maybe after I graduate I'll think about moving to California. We'll just have to see how things work out. Believe me, there's a big part of me that wants to pick up and join you. How is it that you became this free spirit, living a life that everybody thinks about, but hardly anybody ever does?"

"My father was a sociopath. You might say he dug himself into a hole that he saw no escape from. It's much too long to tell. He wound up committing suicide last month. I had already decided to graduate early, but after my dad did that to himself – and us – I just decided to get out of there. My mom actually cooperated."

"I've got a long tether, thank god. Even when my mom was still alive, worry was sort of minimized in our family. When I would leave to do something, Mom and Dad would always say, 'Have fun,' not, 'Be careful.' They taught us, me and my brother, John, to be responsible, but they really encouraged us to be adventurous, too. And all the while they made sure our needs were being met."

"It's great that you appreciate it." Jenny and Kathy talked and talked. Jenny felt closer to Kathy in that short time than she ever had to any friend. At about one in the morning, Kathy gave Jenny an elegant lacy white nightgown to put on. It made her feel very classy, and when she told her so, Kathy insisted that she keep it. Before they crawled into their beds, they decided that the two of them would spend the following day fooling around in Salt Lake City, while Belt transacted his business.

The next morning, Belt said that they could drop him at his meeting place, and Kathy and Jenny could use the rental car. They drove out to the Great Salt Lake and swam in the buoyant, salty water; showered; listened to a pin drop in the Tabernacle; and perused the museum. At the end of the day they knew the names of all the famous Mormons, none of whom were women. That night they ate dinner at the same restaurant where they had been the previous night and this time they opened Belt's bottle of Bordeaux, a Chateau Lafite Rothschild which felt like velvet in Jenny's mouth. They had flaming filet mignon, prepared table-side by a guy who looked as if he would be at home swallowing firey swords in the sideshow of a circus. In Albany, eating had always been a lackluster affair, usually depressing because of her father's behavior; so the festive atmosphere and exquisite food enraptured Jenny. Belt could tell.

"Are you enjoying yourself, Jenny?"

"I'm in heaven! Belt... you're sure Belt is okay?"

"Absolutely."

"I had a very dysfunctional father, so it's been wonderful to watch how you and Kathy interact. You must be very proud of her. I'll keep you posted on what I'm doing."

"Do keep in touch. I can't remember when I have so enjoyed the company of one of Kathy's friends. Occasionally, I have reason to go to California, and if I can pry Kathy away from whatever she's doing, maybe we can visit."

"God, let's hope so." Jenny was sad that this elegant evening and fine company was coming to an end.

Back in their room, Kathy asked, "Do you think I should tell him about the cages incident?"

"I'd keep a lid on it for now, Kath. If there's no backlash in a month or so, you could tell him. That's up to you. No need giving the guy something to worry about."

"Do you have any idea why we're here?"

"Not a clue."

"Well, it's political. Dad's always been an active organizer, and to a certain extent a politician. He's being considered as a future candidate for Governor – in a few years. As he put it when he told me, the republican party has him in its sights. It's kind of hard to believe."

"Wow."

"My feeling exactly."

"My parents were democrats, but to hear my dad talk, every politician from both parties is a dishonest self-serving crook."

"Maybe your dad wasn't so crazy after all. My dad thinks the same thing. He wants to change the image."

"Well my dad wasn't stupid. He was a college professor after all. But he *was* crazy."

Kathy smiled at Jennifer. "By the way, did I ever thank you for saving my life? That was the scariest thing that's ever happened to me and from the initial sighting of the C.C. rapist to the snuff, it was over in about a minute. You're a regular storm, Jenny."

"We've had a fairly compact little friendship, Kath."

"Are you sad that this fragment of your life is ending?"

"Yes. Sad. But as you know, I'm California bound."

ಬಿ

Jenny half expected them to fly her on to California, but instead, Belt wanted to buy her an airplane or train ticket. She was tempted but told him the truth: she was having a good time, meeting interesting people, and learning a lot on this trip. So the next morning they all got up and had breakfast together, loaded up the Hertz Buick, and headed for the airport. Before they got there, they let Jenny out beside a sign that said, Interstate Highway 80, Westbound; she kissed them both good-bye and then stood there crying as they drove away. There on the outskirts of Salt Lake City, the sunshine sparkling in the frost-covered sagebrush, Jenny was alone again.

CHAPTER FOUR

Jenny's eyes were still wet when her next ride came. She didn't even stick her thumb out because it was obvious to her that there was no room for an extra passenger. But they stopped anyway. A green early-post-war Chevy pick-up truck piled so high with stuff that much of it was hanging over the sides of the bed. "Climb on in. Bring the pack in with you, there's no room in back." By Jenny's estimation, there wasn't any room in front either, but she squeezed in. Reluctantly. The cab smelled like an outdoor dog show in the rain. Within five minutes they were up to forty miles per hour, and each time the driver shifted gears, each of the six people that were now in the cab, plus the dog, had to change position.

"Maybe I should get out and wait for someone else to come along. This is really tight."

"It's not much worse than it was with us five plus the dog. I'm Jeff. This here's Tildie, the little lady – ain't she a cutie?" Jeff's mouth opened in a semi-toothy grin. A three- or four-day patchy stubble seemed to dance on his face when he smiled. Tildie *was* cute, a freckled doll-like wife with a baby at her breast. Everybody in the truck was small, they had to be to fit – Jeff looked like he might be tall, but he was thin. "This'n is Jeff Jr., this'n is Tommy, an' the baby is Tillie. Each smiled as they were introduced – even Tillie, whom Tildie took off her breast for a moment to acknowledge the introduction. At 115 pounds, Jenny was probably the heaviest person in the cab. "An' the doggie there is Shep." The doggie looked uncomfortable, especially with Jenny's backpack squished against his side, but everybody else looked right at home.

"Where are you folks going?"

"Reno," they answered in unison – all except Tillie, of course.

"How long of a trip would you say it is from here?"

"Twelve hours, God willin'."

"That's what you said about two hours ago," cried Jeff Jr. in despair. Jeff Sr. laughed. So did Tildie.

"Where you goin', honey?" Jeff asked.

God, if I only knew the name of a town ten miles or so down the road I could bail out of this mess. "Berkeley."

"That in Californie?"

"Yep."

"Long trip ahead a ya." The conversation had to be shouted because the pick-up was so noisy. "They tell me that out here on the salt flats you can drive a hundred miles an hour an' the cops'll never bother ya." Jenny looked at the speedometer and it was up to forty-five, which, from the sound of the engine, was about max. "We have to take 'er kind a slow 'cause a the load we're carryin'. Can ya swim?"

"Sure."

"They tell me that if ya swim in the Great Salt Lake that ya float a lot better than ya do in a reg'lar lake. I don't know why. None a us can swim."

"Well, I went in a couple days ago with a friend. We did float pretty well, I guess."

"Used to have a brother, Roy. He could swim. One time he went down to the river to take a dip and got tangled up with a bunch a snakes. That was the last swim he ever took."

"You mean they bit him?"

"That's what I mean."

"Why didn't he ever swim again? I mean like in a pool or something?"

"After that he couldn't swim any more 'cause he was dead. As far as I'm concerned nothin' but harm can come a swimmin'. If God wanted us to swim he'd a gave us fins instead a hands and feet. Ain't that right Tildie?"

"Jeff, maybe the girl would like somethin' to eat."

"Like som'um to eat, honey?"

"No thanks. I just had breakfast."

"What's yer name, honey?"

"Jenny. Sorry. I should have mentioned it."

"No matter."

Periodically, a foul smell would fill the truck, Jeff would yell, "Shep!" and Jeff, Jr., and Tommy would giggle. "Ever heard of Okies, Jenny?"

"I've heard of the word."

"Yer ridin' with Okies. Ain't that right, Tildie?" He cackled like a goose. "Ever heard a Johnny Cash?"

"Sure. He was one of my favorites."

"He was my other brother. Lucky for him, he never learn't to swim. Mighta wound up like Roy, otherwise."

"Jeff!" Tildie said in a syrupy, scolding tone.

"Did ya ever hear him sing that song, *How High's the Water, Mama*?"

"Sure. I love it."

"He wrote that'n during a flood when we was kids. Water scare't the shit out of 'im. Can't blame 'im. Like I said, he couldn't swim. Plus, as Roy discovered, you never know what might be in the water. About the only time swimmin' can do ya any good anyways is in a flood. Otherwise it'll bring ya nothin' but harm. I was scare't too. We was up on the roof. Roy was there, too. He hadn't taken his last swim yet. In fact he hadn't taken his first one. He hadn't learn't yet. The water was comin' up just like the song says."

"Where were you living?"

"In Oklahoma. Didn't ya hear me say we was Okies?"

"I didn't know what that meant. I'm happy to see you didn't drown. And a good song came out of it. You can't do much better than that, I guess."

"Two foot more and all three of us would a been goners. The water was goin' by fast, and we thought the barn was gonna float away. There was this weather vane on top the barn and we was holdin' on for dear life. Then Johnny started singin' out, 'How high's the water, mama?' Roy an' me laughed till we peed our pants. Roy did anyhow. I didn't."

"I'm surprised you didn't learn to swim after that."

"Roy did," Jeff said, looking over at Jenny, incredulous at her logic. "Look what it did fer him."

"What are you going to Reno for?"

"Find work."

"What do you do?"

"What *did* I do, or what am I *gonna* do?"

"Either one."

"I ran trot lines."

"What's that?"

Jeff cackled again. "Where you been all your life, honey?"

"Albany, New York."

"Trot lines is fishin' lines. One line with a lot a baited hooks hangin' down from it. Catfish takes the bait, ya pull 'em all up, and ya sell 'em to the restaurants."

"I'm surprised you had a job like that if you can't swim."

More cackling. "Ya don't swim. Ya go in a boat."

"Did you wear a life preserver?"

"Sheeit!"

"How come you decided to move?"

"Farmers run me outta bi'ness. Big ol' catfish farms moved in. Acres an' acres a ponds. They could sell three cats to the restaurant for what I needed to get for one. I tried to hire on at one and they didn't want me. Said they needed someone with a edacation. Can't raise cats unless you got a edacation."

"I'll bet you know more about catfish than the people who work there."

"Honey, you ain't as dumb as I thought."

"Jeff, her name is Jenny."

"I'm gonna tell ya som'um about farmed cats, honey. They taste like fish food. Did you ever eat any dog food?"

Shep raised an eyebrow and tried to move but couldn't. Jenny squirmed and moved her backpack a little to try to help him. "No. You mean the canned kind or the dry kind? I never ate either kind."

"The dry kind. I don't expect people would eat the canned kind unless they was pretty hungry. Well, fish food tastes about three or four times as bad as yer dog food. An' the farmed cats taste like the food they feed 'em. Ain't that right, Tildie? Tildie knows. She was the first one t' notice. One night we all went out. Remember that, Junior?"

"Yeah."

"Remember that, Tommy?"

"Yeah."

"We all went out to this restaurant where they'd give ya all the catfish and hush puppies you could eat for a dollar an' six bits. Griff – he ran the place – let the kids eat for nothin' cause he felt bad that he wasn't buyin' from me anymore. Well, he brought us a big ol' platter a cats and a big ol' platter a hush puppies, and Tildie right away says, 'What's that funny smell, Jeff?' An' so we all started sniffin' at everything to see if we could find out what was smellin' so funny. You shoulda seen us, honey. We was like dogs in a restaurant. Ya ever seen them pitchers a dogs playin' poker?"

Jeff waited for an answer, so finally Jenny said, "Yeah, a friend of mine had a couple of those."

"Well, we was dogs in a restaurant. Anyhow, we was all sittin' at our table sniffin' around like dogs, an' then Tildie says, 'It's the catfish!' An' so we all sniff the catfish and sure enough, it's the cats. Ain't that right?"

"That's right." Tildie removed the sleeping Tillie from her breast and pulled her sweatshirt down. Like Jenny, everybody in the truck was wearing a sweatshirt.

"So we all took and put one on our plate, an' we tasted of the son-of-a-bitches, and they tasted a fish food. Cats is normally sweet, but these tasted a the food they was eatin'. Feed, I mean. Pond feed, they call it.

"Did ya ever live in the country, honey?"

"I've lived in the city all my life."

"Well, if ya ever live in the country you'll find that there gets to be more and more rabbits for awhile and then there gets to be more and more foxes for awhile. The foxes catch the rabbits and eat 'em, and when they's so few rabbits that them foxes can't find 'em, the foxes quit havin' babies. Some of 'em die. All of 'em never die, but most of 'em do. The ones that live – honey, they are the ones that are strong and fast and healthy, an' sly, a course. So it starts all over again and they gets to be a lot of rabbits 'cause they ain't many foxes. An' then the foxes start havin' babies again. The off-spring of the rabbits and the foxes is always from the ones that survived the cycle – the strong ones.

"Now then, honey, when they gets to be all those rabbits, do you s'pose them foxes git together and say, 'Hot damn, they's a lot a rabbits now, so we can have us a lot a babies'? Course not, it just happens. It's just like them foxes and rabbits is on a teeterboard." Jeff paused and looked at Jenny. "If you think it's any different with people an' food you'd be wrong. People just haven't started on the down trip yet. And I'll tell ya one more thing. When they start down, it's gonna be a fast trip, and it ain't gonna be the strong, healthy ones that survive, it's gonna be the rich ones. Oh, I think you're gonna be okay, but I'm not so sure about Tillie here. She might see it happen, God help her. This poor child ain't gonna be rich, either. Not unless she figgers out som'um her daddy didn't."

36

Jenny thought of Belt with his miles and miles of farmland, a private plane, and a huge basement full of fancy wine. Can this man with a heart of gold really be poisoning the earth? Can Jeff possess more wisdom than Belt? Was it pure chance that she had been picked up by Jeff after Belt had dropped her off?

"What will you be doing in Reno?"

"Well, honey, first I'm gonna find me some work. Maybe dealin' cards. Then we're gonna get settled somewhere, and when we're all set up, I'll play some poker. It's not just one a yer crackpot schemes. I'm good at poker. I win seventy percent of the time I play. Another way to say it, over the course a time, I come out with about twenty percent more'n I go in with. In a new place with new people, it'll take awhile, but I'll make my money. You don't need a edacation to play poker. Ever been to Reno, honey?"

"Every inch we move is an inch farther west than I've ever been before."

"Well, you'll hear a lot a people say ya either love it or ya hate it. Me, I don't love it and I don't hate it. It's just a place."

"Do you like poker, or is it just like a job to you?"

"Playin' poker is a lot like getting through life. Each card is a challenge. Ya get some good ones. Ya get some bad ones. But ya got t' do the best ya can with ever' one of 'em. The one advantage ya have in poker is that ya can fold the hand. Ya can't do that in life. In life ya got t' play each card. Ya got to do the best ya know how with ever' challenge."

When Jenny had first squeezed into the cab she decided that she would make a short trip of it somehow. She would try to think of excuses to stop as they came to small towns along the way, but, as with the Beltons, she began to feel as if she was part of a family. Jeff talked off and on all the way. The dog kept farting, but it always tickled Junior and

Tommy. When they stopped for gas, Jenny offered to pay for it. Jeff said, "That's sweet a ya. Thanks, honey."

When they got to Sparks, Nevada on the outskirts of Reno, Jeff said, "This is the end a the line for us, honey. Californie is right over them hills there. That's what they call the Donner Pass. When the settlers were comin' through here you might say they stalled out up there. Got into some deep snow. It was pretty grim according to how they tell it. Now the highway goes all the way over the top. Interstate all the way. Dollars to donuts a lot of these skiers ya see are from Californie. You can prob'ly go the rest of the way with one of em. You take care a yourself, honey." No sooner had he said it than Jeff was back behind the wheel and on his way to wherever he was going to stay that night. Jenny watched til the old green pickup truck was out of sight.

CHAPTER FIVE

Now what? It was colder here than it had been in Albany when she started out. She looked around and spotted a Motel 6. She'd got this far for the price of fifty pitches at the batting cages and one tank of gas for Jeff, so she decided to part with the cost of a room, and more important, a hot shower. She knew she smelled like Shep, and she was also hungry, but she'd deal with that in the morning.

When she peered out of her window the next morning there were a couple inches of new snow on the ground. The room was warm and so was the bed, so she stayed where she was until nine-thirty or so. Seldom had Jenny ever felt so good about a decision to treat herself to anything. Still, she knew that she was not yet at her destination, and she was famished, so she dressed, arranged her pack, and ventured out into the light snow.

A short walk along a boardwalk brought her to a large casino advertising a buffet breakfast. She had never seen anything like the array of machines and tables that she had to pass in order to get to the restaurant. After watching a woman play a slot machine for awhile, she dropped a nickel in the one next to the woman and pulled the handle. The wheels rolled around and stopped on two plums and a watermelon. No money came out, and the pictures of the fruits reminded her that she was there to eat, so she paid a cashier and entered the buffet area. Jenny doubted the restaurant made any money on this $2.49 special, even though her foray into gambling made it a $2.54 special. She loaded up her plate with sausages, bacon, gooey looking cinnamon rolls, and corned beef hash.

As she leisurely munched her way though the pile of food she had served herself, Jenny watched the clientele, many of them skiers, moving about – some at the tables, some eating and some playing slot machines. This was a world unlike anything in Albany, New York. The skiers were dressed in bright colored parkas and tight fitting pants of all colors. After finishing her plate, she got more coffee and sat down at a counter in the sports book. A bank of 25 television sets were all tuned into different sports events that the patrons watched with tense excitement. A woman behind the counter asked if she could help Jenny, who thanked her and moved on feeling out of place.

She took her coffee back to the table where she had eaten and sat down. Thinking back over her ride with Jeff's family, she smiled, wondering if the story about the flood was true or not. Unlike her friends, Jenny had been a Johnny Cash fan for most of her life, and she felt she would probably know if he'd ever had a brother named Jeff. Nope Jeff was just a guy with a story. She mused over the way her trip had gone. *Who would be next? What would she learn now? Anything?*

As she looked around at the patronage in the restaurant-casino, the thought occurred to her that she did not have to hurry. Although she had never set a time schedule, if she had, she'd be ahead of it. She was in a warm comfortable setting where she could hang out as long as she wanted to – maybe she could choose her own ride this time rather than accepting the randomness that is a part of hitchhiking. In all the time she'd lived in Albany, she had never met people who had stories like those she had heard on this trip – even if some of them were made up. The older you are the more stories you have, she realized. Most of her acquaintances in Albany were her own age and had the same stories that Jenny herself had.

Her father probably had some that would be interesting – maybe flat out fascinating, but by the time Jenny got old enough to appreciate them, he was such a mental mess that it was in her best interest to keep as much air-space between them as she could. Any conversation was worse than useless.

She continued surveying the crowded casino area. There was a guy who looked a little like Belt. If you look like a guy who's a good guy does that make you a good guy, she wondered. Not necessarily, she guessed. He looked pretty intent on playing machine poker. *If he knew what he was doing he'd get in a real game like Jeff planned to do.*

All the time Jenny was eating, there was a woman sitting alone at a table reading. She was still there. A few cottage fried potatoes remained on her plate and occasionally she would absently stab one with a fork and eat it. She was not dressed for skiing, appeared to be in her mid-forties and wore a sweatshirt with the Cal logo. *Now that would be convenient.* Jenny watched for awhile and decided to go back to the buffet and try some of the cottage fries. She walked by the woman she had been watching, and saw that the book's title was *Coping with Unexpected Adversity.* On an impulse, Jenny stopped at the table.

"Your potatoes looked so good I decided to go get a few myself."

The woman smiled. "They're good."

Jenny tried to think up the next thing she should say but drew a blank. The woman said, "I notice you're toting a back pack around with you. You must be a student."

"Not yet, but as a matter of fact I'm headed for Berkeley to become one."

"Get your potatoes and join me if you'd like."

"Thanks. I was secretly hoping you'd say that."

"Not a well-kept secret. It was fairly clear that you've been sizing me up."

"That's a little embarrassing – very true though. I'll be right back."

Jenny put her plate on the table and retrieved her pack. After she sat down, she told the woman her name.

"My name is Grace. So… I've got a Cal sweatshirt, and I'm reading a book with what might be an intriguing title. And of course the potatoes. What part of sizing me up prompted the introduction?"

"I guess the Cal shirt. Since I'm headed there – well, you know – I figured maybe you'd be a good source of… uh, no, the honest answer is that if there is any chance that you may be going that way yourself any time soon, I was wondering if I could get a ride to Berkeley with you."

"To be perfectly honest, I'm trying to get through some stuff right now that I think I might be more successful processing alone. I'm leaving for there shortly, as a matter of fact, but as I say, I think I'd be better off traveling alone."

No you wouldn't was the first thing that came to Jenny's mind, but she squelched the urge to say it. "Are you sure I'm not in your way right now? I hate it when someone interrupts my reading, and that's just what I did to you."

"I appreciate your honesty about wanting a ride. Do you live here? Are you just visiting, or what?"

"Passing through, actually." Jenny ran through a very abbreviated story of her trip.

"Interesting. You must have graduated early."

"I did. I had to get out of my family, out of my house, out of Albany. In fact out of the eastern US. My dad shot himself a couple weeks ago. Listen, I don't want to get into my troubles. Apparently you've got your own. I really do apologize. I should have let you be."

"Let's get going," Grace said without drama. "Finish your taters and we'll hit the road."

CHAPTER SIX

Jenny buckled herself into Grace's late model Prius and they turned onto westbound I-80. "I'm so grateful you changed your mind that I'm almost afraid to ask why you did," she said.

"Your honesty. Your straight forward answers. Also, you look a little waif-like, if you don't mind my saying so. When you told me what you were up to, I realized I'd hit the bull's eye with that assessment. Of course it also helped that you said you were going to Cal. I don't know whether you're aware of it, but we who go there, or in my case, went there, call it Cal. You'll hear a few people refer to it as Berkeley, but they're the people that don't get it, if you know what I mean."

"How did you like it there – as a student I mean?"

"I loved it. When I was there they had good football and basketball teams which was great because even before I went there I was a Cal fan. I grew up in Marin County right across the bay from the Cal campus."

"What brought you to Reno?"

"I had to attend a conference here. A pesticide conference. That's what's troubling me. Maybe you should tell me a little more about yourself. I could use some distraction."

Jenny told Grace in detail about each of the people she had ridden with on her trip. Each leg of the journey seemed as if it were preordained. Jenny was never one to believe in destiny, and her last experience with religion was not one to strengthen her belief in any aspect of the church. Still, in her relatively young life Jenny had experienced several chains of events that seemed to surpass all odds of being just coincidental. She told Grace that she felt like there was some kind of lesson or message, but she didn't know what it might be.

"It could just be luck. Your experience at the batting cage could have changed the whole trip. Then instead of feeling a sense of awe about it, you'd be cursing your misfortune. The book I'm reading reckons that life experiences can be streaky. Maybe that's so. Maybe it's not. But it sounds like your life was not ideal, or maybe I should say it was beyond challenging before you left Albany. Maybe you were just due for some good things to happen along the way."

"I like that attitude. So your book is saying hang in there during the storm and wait for the sun to shine again?"

"No. It has advice on procedures for remedying problems. The streaky part is only something it mentions. Kind of an aside. I don't think the author could get very far with a book that just tells you to keep a stiff upper lip."

"Yeah. I see what you mean. So anyway, that's me in a nutshell. Was that enough distraction? Do you want to tell me what is troubling you?"

"I must say, I haven't met many people your age who are quite as aware of the ways of the world as you appear to be. I'll tell you my situation, or maybe a simplified form of it and you can tell me what you think I should do."

"Okay. I went to a therapist for a few months – you know, when my dad was giving me headaches – so I'll just sit in the therapy chair for you."

Grace looked over at Jenny and smiled. "You're something else," she said.

"Can you elaborate on that for me, Grace?"

Grace laughed. About then they arrived at the California fruit and vegetable inspection station in Truckee and were waved through after declaring that they didn't have any.

"Okay, Jenny, you're the therapist. Should I call you Jennifer, Miss Lindsey, or Jenny?"

"Whichever you prefer. Of course which name you choose will give me further insight into your persona."

Grace had not felt like laughing for at least a week. Suddenly she felt, if only temporarily, that a weight had been removed from her shoulders. All because she decided to give this waif-like kid a ride. "Okay, Jenny. For now, I'll give you a general synopsis of my immediate problem. If I drive really slowly, we could get into my divorce, my bullying brother and all sorts of juicy stuff, but for now I've got an interesting, albeit depressing professional problem."

"Start at the beginning. I'm serious now. The truth is – and you know this as well as I do – I'm not going to give you advice. But if you tell me what started your trouble, you'll at least hear yourself talking and maybe that will help you work through it."

"Don't be afraid to tell me what you think, Jenny. Sometimes intuition doesn't require the wisdom that comes with age."

"Okay." *This is too bizarre,* thought Jenny.

"I graduated from Cal with a major in zoology. After I got my degree, I went on to an MS. in Chemistry at Cal Tech. Then I came back to Cal and got a PhD in entomology. Do you know what pheromones are?"

"No."

"Well they are organic secretions that are sensed by other individuals of the same species often at a subliminal level, that stimulate certain behavior. The more courses I took, the more I realized how much behavior is caused by pheromones. They can signal danger, attraction, such as sexual readiness, fear, a call to aggregate, all sorts of things. The list goes on and on. So for my dissertation research, I studied pheromones. More specifically, I was able to use certain techniques to extract them from different animals – in my research mostly insects – and analyze their chemical composition. There are machines that are called atomic spectrometers and gas chromatographs that do the chemical analyses, so my main job was to get critters to produce the pheromone or in some cases I found the producing organ and extracted it. Are you following this?"

"Yes, go on. Oh, by the way, how are they sensed?"

"Most often by smell, but there is still some uncertainty about that. Good question."

"Go on, Grace. I'm lovin' this."

"You've probably read about how people can be attracted to certain other people because of the way they smell. Not necessarily perfumes or shave lotions, but natural aromas that are produced organically. Same deal. In humans the smells aren't pheromones, but the attraction phenomenon based on a subliminal sense is analogous. People usually aren't even aware it's happening. Anyway, I became really good at analyzing sexual attractants from insects, certain arachnids, certain small mollusks and so on. I focused on species that are significant pests. Since any pheromones that are produced can only be sensed by individuals of the same species, these wonderful products can be used selectively. If I want to attract the beetle that kills pine trees for example, I can do that without attracting any other species of beetle – the ladybird bird beetle, for example. Can you see where I'm going with this?

"Where I see you going is to zillions of dollars, which I do not really see as a problem."

"Well, Jennifer, you're right on target. I started a business that was going to replace almost all of the insecticides that are being sold today, and replace them with products that would not involve poisons. When I started, there were already some traps on the market, but I developed four different ways to use pheromones to eliminate populations of pests without using poisons of any kind."

"Still no problem that I can detect."

"Well, that's next." They were traveling through deep drifts along the highway. Skiers and snowboarders were visible enjoying a suddenly bright sunny day in the resorts near the freeway. "Were you aware that the 1960 Winter Olympics were held right over there at Squaw Valley?" Grace asked.

"Hah! I am a fan of the Winter Olympics, but you might want to check with my grandpa about that one. That was well before my time."

"Well, yeah, of course. It was before my time, too. But I know because I'm a Californian, and because I occasionally ski there. Anyway, that's where they were. You can't see it from here, but it's right over there."

"Are you running into some difficulty talking about the problem," Grace?

"No, sorry. The problem is actually two problems. One is that my chief scientist, who knew all my proprietary secrets, quit a couple weeks ago." Grace glanced over at Jenny to see if she could get a read on whether Jenny grasped the significance of her statement.

"Did you have patents?"

"Some pending, but some of the techniques involved in producing these products are the real breakthrough, and this guy knew them all."

"You used a couple of past tenses there. Was that on purpose?"

"Yes. The guy has disappeared. Right now the cops are treating it as a missing persons case, but I think he was murdered."

CHAPTER SEVEN

Jenny jerked around in her seat. "What?"

"Yeah, murdered. I can't say for sure. But that's what I think. I'm also worried that I could be next."

"Oh my god, Grace, I'm thinking you should find a real therapist. Not only that. You should go to the cops, move, quit going to pesticide conferences, quit offering rides to strangers... let's see, what else?"

"I think you're starting to get it why I'm troubled."

"No doubt about that. Is there anything in that book of yours that is going to guide you through this, uh... situation you're in?"

"Murder of a colleague is not covered. The author talks about things like getting fired, getting jilted, dealing with a financial crisis, death of a loved one. Stuff like that. No colleague murders. Obviously this author missed a key 'unexpected adversity.' He actually does advocate optimism as a solution. I do like to think of myself as an optimist; in fact, it's something I like about myself. But as advice coming out of a book that's supposed to teach you how to cope, it's bullshit. How am I supposed to apply that in this situation? Just make an assumption that it won't happen to me? Give me a break.

"When I was a student, I had a job one summer on a forest fire crew. There was this guy on the crew who liked me and we emailed back and forth for awhile after that summer. In one of his emails he talked about a certain precarious situation that we'd encountered on a fire and then said, 'What are you gonna do? Oh well. Just go on, I guess.' I still smile about the profound thinking that went into that conclusion.

"Anyway, that's about how useful my book has been. At least in my case. If I get into a financial crisis I'll be okay. By the way, the author doesn't even have anything to say about dad's shooting themselves. I guess it wouldn't do you much good either."

Jenny smiled. Even if Grace hadn't solved anything, she at least was able to find some humor in her situation. Jenny realized that once again she had defied all odds and found another great friendship on her trek across the country. "So Grace, what are you going to do?"

"Just go on, I guess."

"Hey, it's good you're past your gloom, but don't you think you should make a plan?"

"Well yeah. That's what *you're* supposed to do. You're the therapist after all."

"Grace, I'm serious. If your guy really was murdered, why do you think you might be next?"

"Because before this guy – my chief scientist, Roscoe was his name – quit, he told me that he'd got a telephone call from one of the big-name pesticide companies advising him to close down our operation. I think the company thought he was the boss. Anyway, it wasn't just a suggestion. It was a threat. Roscoe didn't say it, but I'm pretty sure it was a death threat. He told me about the call and that he was, in his words, scared shitless. I'm not sure what he thought that quitting would accomplish, but anyway that's what he did."

"So you're thinking is that if you're right, and you go on making and marketing your products, you're going to be in danger."

"Yep. That's what I think. Makes sense, don't you think. Actually, we haven't got them on the market yet, but we're close."

"Which company threatened him?"

"They didn't tell him. Whoever it was that called said it would make a lot of people happy if he would shut down his production facility. Three months ago we rented a warehouse in Richmond – that's a city a few miles north of Berkeley – and invested in a bunch of equipment. Everything about this situation wreaks with fear and uncertainty."

"Okay. I've asked you this twice already. Have you got any ideas about what you might do?"

"Well, I *have* gone to the police. As I told you, they are calling it a missing persons case. I'm not sure they believed my story. First of all, I think the guy I talked to was skeptical that my product was that good. I mean the companies that dominate the pesticide market are huge. The cop had a hard time believing that I posed enough of a threat to ruffle the feathers of such huge companies. For one thing, I don't think I explained the pheromone concept very well. Beyond talking to the police, I can't think of anything else to do."

"What do you think Roscoe is going to do? I mean why did he quit? It doesn't seem like that accomplishes anything. And if he truly got murdered, it didn't. One thing that comes to mind is that if he's alive and really is scared, it doesn't matter if he knows your proprietary secrets. It doesn't seem too likely that he's going to start up production himself."

"In fact, he couldn't. He doesn't know every step of the process. But he does know the concept and some of the secrets that enable the formulations; so theoretically he could just figure out what else is involved in producing the product.

"The only thing I really know is what he told me. Maybe he just made up that story. It wouldn't be hard to disappear and set up a plant somewhere and start his own research to fill in the gaps in his knowledge.. I saw this as a huge deal, both because of the specificity of my products and the fact that they are environmentally benign. So I put out a lot of press releases to publicize my stuff. The newspapers and on-line media services were interested, so I got a lot of press – free advertising, as it were. If Roscoe made up the story he told me, and could figure out how to combine the pheromones correctly with the control mechanisms, he would derive those same benefits from the publicity. I'm just so mad about the whole quandary I'm in. If Roscoe got murdered, I'd feel awful. He was a strange guy but good worker. But you never want to see a guy get killed. My moods about this deal are all over the place.

"Roscoe apparently comes from some money, so if he really was going to try to make these products himself, he could mobilize pretty quickly. It took me years to get loans on such a speculative venture. Imagine how I feel – sad if he's been murdered, but angry at him if he just up and quit – especially if he's going to start up his own business using what I taught him. And then there's the added wrinkle that if he got murdered they may decide to take me out, too, so fear factors in."

"Yeah, I see what you mean. Your situation is way more complex than having your father blow his brains out – especially if the father is a sociopath, and he and everybody who knew him is better off if he's dead. My experience was a sudden blow, to be sure; but no residual worries. Your situ has too many variables and unknowns."

CHAPTER EIGHT

Jenny and Grace stopped in Auburn for a Mexican lunch. Jenny had filled her plate so full at the casino buffet in Sparks that she was still not very hungry, so she ordered a chicken tostada. Grace ordered enchiladas which were served with rice and beans loaded up with cheese. As they ate, Jenny studied Grace's facial features – very young looking but probably forty, she guessed. Her blue eyes still reflected a hint of her distress over the events she had been recounting with Jenny, but the creases at the corners suggested that she probably smiled more than she frowned. She looked like a happy, self-satisfied woman who was a little tired. Of course she looked tired. She was coping with a very unsettling conundrum.

As Jenny studied Grace, she could tell that Grace was doing the same to her. *Maybe she's thinking I'm wise beyond my years,* she thought – and hoped. After they had eaten in silence for awhile, Grace said, "Jenny, so far you've been a good therapist. I think we're making progress but there's still a road ahead. Maybe a long one."

"Berkeley can't be more than a couple more hours from here. Maybe we need to set up an appointment schedule," Jenny said, half seriously. Then "seriously, if you decided not to get professional help, I think that by just talking we can define the components of the problem and discuss what the remedy options might be."

"You talk like you do this all the time."

"My crazy dad used to parse everything. If he hadn't been nuts, he probably would have been interesting. Anyway, he was a master at separating almost any aspect of life into the elements that comprised it. He was always saying, 'Parsing isn't just for sentences.' He thought that in order to understand anything you had to know what it was made of."

"It really is too bad that he had a mental disorder. He sounds like he must have been interesting during his saner moments."

"A lot of his students thought he was cool. Especially some of the women, who discovered that they could get extra credit by scheduling office visits. You know, I tell people that he was crazy, or nuts, but the truth is that he knew what he was doing. He had no conscience. I guess you'd call him a sociopath. My guess is that when he killed himself it wasn't because he felt guilty, but because he had been exposed to the university and church communities and knew that he was about to get fired and ostracized. For a long time he was buddies with the priest. At home, he would say he didn't like Fr. Mark, but that there were benefits to be derived from being his companion. He was always looking for easy ways to get ahead. Things he could do that would give him some advantage."

"I must say, Jenny, for somebody that looks a little lost, you have quite an array of stories to tell."

"Funny you should say that because only this morning I was thinking about the stories I'd heard on this trip and kind of concluded that I wasn't old enough to have a good supply. I guess that I have never taken time to parse my life, as my father would call it. I just thought of it as my life. Not a series of events that could be tales to tell."

The two women declined dessert and asked for the check, which Grace graciously paid. "Partial payment for your counseling services," she said.

As they dropped down toward Sacramento they could see a lake of fog covering the city. Grace explained that it was tule fog, a winter phenomenon in that area.

Jenny showed minimal interest because she was gearing up for their next session. "Tell me a little bit about Roscoe," she said.

"I liked Roscoe, but as I think back over the time I knew him there are some things that don't quite fall into place. When I was working on my PhD at Cal, I was a teaching assistant. Roscoe was an excellent student, almost brilliant I used to think, and I encouraged him to go on to at least a masters; but he had had enough of school so he got a job in a lab on campus where they were doing cancer research using guinea pigs.

"When I finally got started and interviewed him for a job, I asked him what he was doing up there. He explained the procedures, the concept, the hypotheses, and the research design so clearly that I hired him on the spot. But after he had worked with me for awhile he told me that cancer built character and in fact all disease should just be allowed to run their course. I asked him why he thought that, and he told me that the people who deal with personal crises are stronger. I was flabbergasted, and told him he was deranged. You should have seen him then. Talk about ballistic!

"When we got my processing plant under way, he caught on to the procedures very quickly and occasionally had valid ideas to streamline projects, or improve them in other ways. But then I discovered that he sometimes conducted little experiments of his own. Curiosity stuff that had no bearing on what we were doing."

"Was that good or bad? Did he do it on his time or yours?"

"He did it on company time, so it was bad."

"Did you talk to him about it?"

"Yes, a few times. He would say that it was like a part of his education, that he was making himself a more valuable employee and that over time, his recreational use of our time and facility would accrue benefits to our production. He would say that without saying what those benefits might be."

"Let's see, does that sound anything like my father?"

"Well, I don't know. How do you mean?"

"My dad befriended the priest for the benefits that might accrue. He never said what they might be."

"I can't believe it Jenny. How did I miss that?"

"That you missed it isn't as important as what it means – about Roscoe."

"Roscoe wasn't a sociopath."

"He stole time and used your equipment for personal gain rationalized it by saying it was your gain."

Grace's eyes shifted to the left. "The amount of time wasn't significant."

"Significant enough to mention when you were telling me about his faults."

"God, Jenny you should be an interrogator."

"The more we talk about this, the more I'm beginning to see that I'm not really counseling you. That's pretty obvious because I don't have any training. But we are working on a mystery together. To tell you the truth, I'm dying to propose that we team up in our own effort to figure out what's going on. In other words, there are some mysteries that need solving and I would like to be involved with solving them – together with you, of course. The only thing is, I'm only a girl – untrained in any investigative techniques – but one who was always under scrutiny in her own home. One who had to succeed in a prison camp of sorts, so I have some of the intelligence I gained from that. The other thing is that I'm about to be a college student, which I assume will take up quite a bit of my time."

"I can already tell that the way you approach a problem should mesh pretty well with my way of looking at them.

Maybe we can discover some answers before you start school. Where will you be staying?"

Your house, of course. "I don't know. I've been assigned to a dorm, but I don't know where it is yet."

"You can stay at my place until you move into the dorm."

"Wow, are you sure? I should warn you that I still have a lot of adolescent traits. I probably don't need to explain it, but I get excited, pushy, sometimes even arrogant. Don't be afraid to put me down. It's something I'm used to and really do need occasionally."

"I think my book has something about how to cope with that."

"So does that mean we're going to continue to sort out the elements of your conundrum and solve the mysteries that they present?"

"I'd rather think of it more informally than that, Jenny, but sure – I do think we're making some progress."

"Yippee! I love it."

"If my ex and I had had kids, the oldest would be about your age now. This is a nice little alliance for me."

"Me, too, obviously. One question: do you think we're safe in your home?"

"I hadn't thought of that, but I should think so."

"I think Roscoe's alive, Grace. If I'm right, then we're safe because it means he wasn't murdered, and you aren't next."

"Why do you think that?"

"That's a good question with a bad answer. It's just a feeling – an intuition."

"If you're wrong, there are two possibilities: one, either I'm next – that is, the competition – which we assume is the murderer – doesn't believe that our product is doomed until they take me out, or two, I'm not next – that is, the murderer thinks he's snuffed their competition with one murder. In the latter case, which is possible, they might not believe that I know how to make any of this stuff."

"Now you're evaluating your situation the way my dad used to. He would actually structure situations on paper – something like a decision tree. So my suggestion to you is to try to break down your dilemma into its components and see if there are separate elements to the components. I used to hate when my dad would make me go through something like that when I would ask him if I could go to the movies with my boyfriend. Imagine. Parsing something as simple as a date. But I think we can work out something that might help to find courses of action as more information comes available."

"It's a better idea than the author of my book came up with."

CHAPTER NINE

Grace lived in a small, but elegantly appointed house in the Berkeley hills just west of Tilden Park. The view of San Francisco Bay and the Golden Gate were spectacular. The University of California campus and the prominent Campanile, its tall carillon tower, were visible through the trees looking southwest. The two new acquaintances sat on the front porch watching the sun disappear into the Pacific. Grace opened a bottle of Cabernet Sauvignon and asked Jenny if she would like a soda, or Snapple. Jenny sheepishly told Grace that the future governor of Iowa had offered her a French Bordeaux and she would like to compare the California version to it if Grace would approve. Grace, again a bit taken aback by this young lady, poured a glass of the Cabernet for Jenny.

"Thanks, Grace. I won't make a habit of this."

"Good."

Jenny was overcome with excitement and reverence for the events that had transpired over the last six days leading up to this moment. A part of her wanted to act how she thought a sophisticated adult should, sipping the wine, carefully noting its flavors, and admiring the magnificent view. But another part of her was so intrigued by the mystery that they were working on together that she wanted to resume that discussion.

Jenny told Grace the wine was smooth with nice tannins that gave it an astringency and fullness that she really liked.

She knew little of what her comments meant, but had heard stuff like that at the dinner table at home –especially when they had people over for dinner.

Something about the comment made Grace wonder if Jenny was going to turn out like her father.

Quickly aware of the way Grace was looking at her, Jenny said, "Sorry. I just repeated some stuff I've heard. It is good though. Thanks."

"Well, I'm glad that you were overcome with the need to be honest. Remember, that's what got you a ride."

"Can I show you something I worked on while we were driving?" Jenny asked. It's an outline that I think will help us know what information we have and what we don't. I was just thinking it might be a starting point. We can use it or not, whatever you think."

"Well, Jenny, I thought we might let this thing rest until tomorrow, but why don't you show me what you've got?"

"This is what I have so far. We can keep adding or taking things off as we get more information." She showed the brief outline to Grace.

I. Factual Data
  A. Roscoe disappeared
  B. Roscoe used lab equipment, supplies, and work-time for something personal
  C. Police regard disappearance as missing persons case
  D. Roscoe told Grace that he had received a threatening call
  E. Roscoe is educated, qualified chemist, skilled in pheromone technology
  F. Roscoe has money
II. Unknowns = Assumptions to consider
  A. Roscoe received threatening call
  B. Roscoe did not receive call
III. Possible reasons for disappearance

A. Assuming Roscoe got call
1. Who made the call
a. Why = was it really threatening as he said
2. Reasons for disappearance
a. Murdered – body disposed of
b. Scared and hiding
c. Kidnapped
B. Assuming Roscoe didn't get call and made up the story
???

Grace was amazed. "I didn't even know you had done that. You were talking with me all the way."

"It might be incomplete. For example I couldn't think of anything to list under III. B., the last entry. There are probably lots of possibilities. Maybe he just got sick of the job and took off."

"Yeah, but he would have told me if he was going to do that. I did think of it, but the reason I'm so worried is that I'm pretty sure he would have talked it over with me."

"First you said he would have, and then you said he probably would have. So we're not sure."

"Okay. I'll give you this one."

"Here's the problem, Grace. There are so many possibilities here that it would be impossible to list them all. For now let's just put two: 1. He did something flaky; and 2. He's up to something. One could be practically anything. What's his hobby for example?"

"He likes to fish; I know that."

Jenny's skin tingled for a minute, not because it was a clue of any kind, but because fishing had been a topic of conversation in the rides she got with Mike and Jeff.

Grace noticed Jenny's start. "Does that mean something? It looked like you had a revelation."

"Oh, no. It just fits into the unlikely pattern of my trip. Remember I told you that Mike's dad was a commercial fisherman? Well Jeff was, too. He ran trot lines. I never heard of them, but he explained how they work. Just a weird coincidence, that's all."

"That's life in the Western US.," Grace said. Sport fishing is huge out here. That's not to say that it isn't important in the east. And it's not to say it's not a coincidence. Just a fact."

"Let's talk a little more about Roscoe. You said he was your student for awhile."

"Not really my student. I was a T.A., and he was in a class or two that I taught. I know he was an excellent student."

"What's his last name, by the way?"

"Toth."

Jenny stood up. "No fucking way."

"What? Did I hear you right? Was that you who said that?"

"You heard me right. And it was I who said it."

"Well... I'm speechless. You might have to explain that one."

"Did your job application ask for any I.D.? Social Security, for example?"

"As I remember there was a photocopy of his driver's license. I have no reason to doubt his name."

Jenny said, "I'll be right back," and went into the guest bedroom where she had left her pack. When she returned she asked Grace "Have you ever heard of Lazlo Toth?"

"No who's he?"

"Well the real live Lazlo Toth was the guy who attacked Michelangelo's Pietà in the Sistine Chapel. But a guy you may have heard of adopted that name for a book called *The Lazlo Letters*. Did you ever see Father Guido Sarducci on Saturday Night Live?"

"Of course. That was awhile back, but the guy was a riot."

"Well he was portrayed by a guy named Don Novello who penned *The Lazlo Letters*, which is also a riot. It's a bunch of actual strange and funny letters that he wrote to US. Presidents – especially Nixon, and to corporate CEOs, cabinet members, and all kinds of people I can't remember. He got answers to most of them and it's all in his book. My mom used to read it to us aloud to lighten the mood when my dad was getting out of hand."

"What's that got to do with Roscoe? I mean there can't be just one Toth in the world. I don't get your agitation."

Jenny showed Grace her fake driver's license.

"What in god's name is that? Where did you get it?"

"It's a fake I.D. and I got it from a friend."

"Why?"

"A guy I used to know just gave it to me. He's a friend of a former boyfriend of mine. I don't know why he gave it to me, and I don't know why he picked the name Amy Toth; maybe Toth is a favorite name for license forgers. That doesn't seem likely, either. I just don't get it. Anyway, we have a data point that we wouldn't have if you hadn't changed your mind and given me a ride."

"I don't get it either. If it's a coincidence it's an unlikely one to be sure. I must say, it sheds some suspicion on Roscoe. I hate to say that, because Roscoe is a good guy."

As Grace pondered her initial evaluation and trust of Roscoe, she saw that Jenny was frantically writing stuff in her notebook. In spite of a heightened intrigue over this situation that only this morning had caused her a grisly combination of fear, sadness, and even depression, she was overcome with weariness.

"First priority," Jenny said. "We've got to find out as much as we can about Roscoe. You must know more than you've told me. Let's start with what you know."

"Jenny, I've had it. Tomorrow we can talk about this some more, or we can forget the whole thing and just hole up here for awhile. But I'm done. I was a mess before you even came along, and although you have brought some interesting ideas to bear, I'm done. I'm off to bed. You know where your bedroom is. Stay up as long as you want, but I'm through. Good night, my dear."

CHAPTER TEN

Jenny did not stay up. Although she thought she was wired, she crawled into the guest bed and went to sleep almost instantly in spite of trying to stay awake considering the next steps. It was 9:00 when she heard noises in the kitchen and smelled coffee. One to enjoy the half hour or so between waking up and actually arising, on this morning, Jenny was up, showered and dressed in nothing flat. Grace was ready with a cup of coffee when Jenny entered the kitchen. "I know you drink coffee because you had a mug of it in your hand when I first saw you yesterday."

"Yep. Eighty percent of teenagers drink the stuff. What's that mean, do you suppose?"

"We've got enough to think about without trying to reason out that statistic. How do you happen to have that number at the ready?"

"Health and sex education. All kinds of useful facts."

"Any germane to our investigation?"

"I'd say, no. Although you never know what fact might help solve a case."

"How long did you stay up last night."

"About 30 seconds longer than you did."

"So no further progress to report."

"Sorry to say you are correct."

"I've got some scrambled eggs and toast ready if you want."

"I don't want to be rude, but do you have any cereal? I'm not a big fan of eggs."

"Cornflakes and Grape nuts."

"I'll go with the Grape nuts. Why do you suppose they're called that?"

"Same answer as to why so many teenagers drink coffee. Let's stick to the mysteries at hand."

"Well, actually if we knew the answer, it might be more interesting than the answer to why teenagers drink so much coffee."

"If we had had this conversation yesterday morning, I wouldn't have given you a ride."

"Maybe we should get on with figuring out more about Roscoe – more about the guy and why he's gone missing."

"After breakfast, my dear."

൭

After finishing her second mug, Jenny said, "I'm itching to get on with this, but what about your job? Do you need to go to work? Do you have any other employees that you need to... um, boss around?"

"No. Roscoe was my only staff. We're still in development. When we start production, we'll need more. Actually, I have already posted job announcements around campus, because I'm pretty sure we can gear up for production within six months or so."

"So you don't need to go to your lab, or plant, or whatever it is, today?"

"No. We could, if you'd like to see it."

"I would, of course, but maybe not today. I want you to tell me more stuff about Roscoe. Where did his money come from, for example?"

"Let me think. I know he's from Oregon. I'm pretty sure he told me his parents have a wheat farm up there somewhere. Dufus, or something like that. It's a couple thousand acres of wheat. Maybe more. I just remember it seemed like a lot of land to own. He was proud of the fact that his family owned a water right and consequently produced considerably more than most of the other growers in the vicinity."

"So he could have gone there. Maybe they need him to help with the harvest."

"He told me he didn't like the work on the wheat farm. He really did like the spectral analyses and experimentation that we were doing in the lab. He's a brainy guy. Fairly non-athletic I'd say. Maybe a little lazy." Grace paused a moment. "You know, I liked and trusted this guy so much that maybe I tended to overlook some things that I should have corrected."

"Do you have any idea what he was doing with your lab equipment? What his purpose was, I mean?"

"No. That's something I'm still curious about."

"What was his major?"

"Organic chem. At least that's what he told me. I never saw a degree, and to be honest I don't think he ever graduated. He talked some about an ecology course, and I remember he talked about an ichthyology course where the professor took everyone in the small class on a fishing trip somewhere out by the Farallon Islands."

"Ichthyology is fish science?"

"It focuses mainly on classification. I never took it. There may be some aspects of fishery biology. I'm not sure."

"One thing I didn't tell you when I talked about my first ride – remember Mike in the big rig?"

"Yes."

"Well Mike's dad was a commercial salmon fisherman. Mike told me a bunch of stuff about salmon that I never knew. It was pretty fascinating stuff. The miraculous part is that they return to spawn in the same part of the same river where they hatched out. It's based on scent. It's kind of like the pheromones you were talking about, except that salmon detect smell in the water.

"Anyway," Jenny continued, "this isn't getting us very far in our case – I'm just going to call this a case from now on. So, well, I'm thinking it might be time to start a new conversation."

"I agree. Where would you go at this juncture?"

"How about telling me about your contact with the police department?"

"Okay. That seems logical. Actually, the way they responded at the police department is the one thing in this whole series of events, that made me the maddest. To this point, we've figured out a few things that might cast some suspicion on Roscoe, but when I talked to the cops I had pretty good reason to believe that he'd been murdered and that my own life was in danger. They just said that they'd alert the personnel in the department that deals with missing persons and they would pursue any leads that came in. I said something like, 'Is that the best that you can do?' and the guy said, 'What do you suggest?' Well, obviously, I don't know anything about investigating murders or any other kind of crime, so I said, 'You're the detective. Aren't you supposed to be the one that figures out what to do?' The guy told me that something like ninety percent of missing persons are only missing for a day or less, and that about one in a hundred turn out to be murders. I'm still pissed about the uncooperative – even rude treatment."

"It sounds to me like that's going to be a dead end, Grace. Anyway, I've got kind of a wild idea. Maybe we should try to find out where Dufus is and go up there. Maybe the guy just got homesick and went home."

"Homesick! He's been at Cal for four years, and another few years working in Berkeley and Richmond. This is his home."

"Well, maybe he went up there for some other reason. I think we should go up to Dufus. I wonder where the hell it is."

"That shouldn't be to hard to find out. Jenny, as you can see, I've been successful enough with banks and venture capitalists to live comfortably, but there isn't a whole lot left over, and I have to send progress reports to my creditors. I really can't afford to go flying around looking for Roscoe. Anyway, I'm not sure it would be good use of our time. It reminds me of *Where's Waldo,* which is one step down from those children's drawings where you have two similar pictures and you spend an hour looking for differences. I just don't see what we could learn in Dufus."

"Grace, don't you ever watch detective movies or read mysteries? The first thing you do in an investigation is talk to people who knew the subject of interest. We've got to head up to Dufus. I'm pretty sure that if I tell my mom that I made it to Berkeley, and what I'm involved in, and that my best friend is a 40-year-old PhD, she'll send me some buckage. Anyway, if you're next in line to be snuffed, we shouldn't be here. They'd find you and off you just like that.

"My dad had a fairly huge life insurance policy that he'd had for years. It was through SUNY. Mom told me that suicide benefits were payable after the policy had been in effect for two years, so she's going to be fat. I need to call her anyway. I'll just slip in a request of a little extra cash."

"My god, Jenny, every idea you come up with blows me away. Go ahead and call your mom. As you say, you owe her that. If she'll send you some money, we'll think about heading north. This is my deal. If you can help a little with gas it would be nice, but I can afford a few days off and a few expenses. You'd faint if I told you how much money is in my lab. Luckily it isn't all mine."

"Yippee." Grace, you are so cool. When do we leave?"
"Let's spend the day prepping and leave tomorrow. If you don't mind my saying it, your wardrobe is a little sparse. If your mom wires money to you, maybe you should look into

some supplemental clothing. By the way I'm 43 years old. Not that it matters, I guess."

Ↄ

Jenny got up from the kitchen table and adjourned to the front room. After a few minutes, she called out, "Grace."

"Yes?"

"It's Dufur."

"What's Dufur?"

"The town in Oregon. I just looked it up on your cell phone. Sorry. I should have asked first."

CHAPTER ELEVEN

Downtown Berkeley was alive with people even though it was drizzling lightly, and Jenny took it all in with great fascination. Grace drove her down Bancroft Way pointing to landmarks as they passed – Sather Gate, several book stores, restaurants, and a few clothing stores. Their destination was the Richmond Costco, but Grace used the moment to give Jenny a brief tour of the sights and commerce of Berkeley, including famous Telegraph Avenue.

Jenny's mom had been delighted and relieved to get the call from Jenny, who spent the better part of an hour talking about her trip west. As the call went on and her mother became more and more enthusiastic about Jenny's tales (not including the Cornfield Cages Caper – which Jenny thought was best omitted), Jenny felt a reluctance to ask for money. But she knew she needed it, and worked it into her expertly spun narrative of the mystery of Roscoe Toth. So when she and Grace arrived at Costco, Jenny had enough to outfit herself not only for the trip, but to get her by when she started classes. Jenny bought a good array of stuff in part with guidance from Grace, and at the end still had a little over $200 to add to the $170 or so that was left from her original $200. She felt flush and assured Grace that she was not going to be a burden on this trip.

"You have not been a burden, Jen. The way you have analyzed this situation has been logical and enlightening. It has relieved me somewhat of both the fear and worry I was experiencing. Burden? No way."

Back at Grace's house they got a road map and studied the route to Dufur. "It would be a long drive if we were to do it in a day. It looks like around 600 miles. We can google the best way to go, but it looks like Bend would be a good stopping place if we get road-weary. I've been up as far as Bend a few times, and it's a nice drive. There's a great ski area there at Mt. Bachelor. We'll be driving up through the Sacramento Valley. The highway follows the Sacramento River most of the way up to Mt. Shasta.

"We've mentioned salmon a couple of times. I know that the Sacramento is the main corridor for salmon spawning in California. Unfortunately, there's a dam at Redding that stops the run. I think there's a hatchery there, but I've heard it hasn't worked out so well."

"Mike told me about a dam that blocked salmon. I think it was on the Columbia River. I'm glad you decided it would be worth it to make this trip. I'm stoked."

"I'm not stoked, but I'm glad you're going with me. I'm glad I gave you a ride from Sparks. I have benefited from your encouragement."

"By the way, we're not going to get road-weary, Grace. We don't have time to make this a leisurely sight-seeing trip. You've got to keep your project in gear, and I have to make it back in time to start classes. Plus, we've got to figure out if Roscoe is alive or dead."

"I expect you're right about that," Grace agreed.

"My god, you may have to find someone to replace Roscoe. From what you said there probably aren't too many people around who are qualified."

"I don't think it'll be hard to find a replacement. Most chemists are familiar with using spectrometers and gas chromatographs. I'm pretty sure that Roscoe never learned how I'm able to get different insects to produce different pheromones. That's the top-secret part of my research and pest control capabilities. As for Roscoe, he'd have to come crawling back with a pretty good story for me to even think about taking him back. Jeez, Jenny, look what he's done to me. And you."

"Actually, I kind of like what he's done with my life. This is exciting. But if it's true that he doesn't know how to extract the pheromones, do you really have to worry that he could start up his own business and compete with you?"

"No, probably not. The trouble is I'm not entirely sure that he doesn't know how I do it. Maybe he does." Grace paused, thinking. "But I think he doesn't. Although, it could be what he was trying to do when he strayed from what he was supposed to be doing. I don't know. I just don't know."

"Hopefully, we'll get some answers tomorrow. Maybe not tomorrow, but soon."

CHAPTER TWELVE

The next morning was clear and cold, but within a couple of miles, the Prius was warm. Jenny had bought a pair of "stylin' shades" at Costco, and it was a day to show them off. Grace dressed in a workout outfit, which is the only thing Jenny had ever seen her wear.

"Were you ever an athlete? I'm asking because you have such a trim body and because of the outfit you wear all the time."

"I played tennis at Cal. I still play when I have time."

"God. You have to get your business off the ground. You'll be able to buy your own tennis court."

"I love your enthusiasm, Jenny. That's how I was when I first started experimenting and got some promising results. Lately, I'm sinking in gloom."

"Something else besides the Roscoe case?"

"Oh, that's the main thing. The finances are getting harder to come by and a couple of personal issues with the ex. Nothing to talk about. Or I should say, nothing that I want to talk about."

"Okay. I won't ask you about anything gloomy. You can tell me stuff about what we see on this trip."

As they crossed the Carquinez Bridge, Grace pointed out that it was a narrow part of the bay and that upstream was the Sacramento River delta. As briefly as possible, she explained that in the process of pumping river water from the delta to arid southern California, the flows often were reversed in the delta. Since downstream migrant salmon cue on flow direction they often become confused and wind up at the pumping stations instead of the ocean.

"What happens then?" Jenny inquired.

"There are screens there, but they are ineffective. Most of the little baby salmon get ground up by the pumps."

Jenny felt revulsed. "What a sad fate."

Grace knew that if you added the value of the salmon catch to the fisherman, the buyer, the wholesaler, the retailer, plus all the costs involved in building and outfitting fishing vessels that you would come up with a major contribution to the economy. She couldn't remember the number, but told Jenny that it was enormous. Jenny listened with rapt attention.

The trip went fast as the conversation shifted between commentary about the scenery and chit chat about Jenny's days in high school. Jenny was awed by Mt. Shasta, which Grace described as the southern-most mountain in the Cascades and the second tallest after Mt. Rainier.

"We'll get a great view of the central Cascades as we drive through Bend," Grace told her.

"Are you ever called Gracie?" Jenny asked.

"Always as a kid."

"I like that. If I do it from time to time, I hope you wouldn't be insulted."

"I'll try to let it pass."

"Would you mind if I used your cellphone, Gracie?"

"What do you have in mind?"

"I want to look up something on line."

"Yes. I mind. When we stop to eat, which will be soon, you can use it. We'll make sure that where we stop has wi-fi."

"Okay. Just wondering."

When they got to Weed, Grace suggested they have lunch at the Hi-Lo Cafe. After they were seated, Grace took out her phone and handed it to Jenny. They have free wi-fi here. Find out how to get on line if that's what you have in mind, because I have a very low data use threshold."

They ordered lunch and asked for prompt service. "It's always prompt," said the silver haired waitress through heavy bright-red lipstick. The voice was thick with years of cigarettes. But prompt the service was. Jenny managed to eat and read at the same time, paying no attention to Grace, who wondered if she'd seen the last of the energetic Jenny – the Jenny that she had grown to care and feel compassion for. Grace had planned to buy lunch for both of them, but when Jenny offered, she acquiesced. Without mentioning it to Jenny, it was because Jenny's attention to the cell phone had annoyed Grace. She would even up the balance sheet, but for now, she hoped that Jenny would learn something. No words were ever exchanged about the incident.

From Weed, they headed north on the two-lane road to Doris, California and Klamath Falls, Oregon. The panorama was sagebrush, juniper, sparse desert grasses and barely visible lava flows from ancient Shasta eruptions. Again, Jenny was captivated by scenery that she'd never seen. Nevertheless, she had been silent since they'd left the Hi-Lo Cafe, and eventually Grace began to wonder if she had done something that upset Jenny. "Are you okay?" she inquired.

"Yeah." After a long pause she added, "Thanks."

After another twenty minutes had passed with no further conversation, Grace grew worried. "What's up?" she said.

"There is something," Jenny replied.

"No better time than now to get it out. By tomorrow we'll be working on our case."

"I found an article on line that's of interest. I left it on your phone, and if you want, I'll read it."

"Well, from the way you're sulking, it seems like that's the right thing to do." She handed the phone to Jenny.

"It's a newspaper article from the Ames, Iowa Tribune."

75

"The Ames Tribune is an unlikely source of interest to you, Jenny, but I remember Ames is where you made friends with the student whose father was a politician."

"That's right. There's a part of that stay that I didn't tell you about. I haven't told anyone, and I told my friend Kathy that she shouldn't tell anyone."

Grace sensed Jenny's anxiety. "You can tell me."

"Grace, I killed a man."

Grace felt her face blanch. She knew that she needed to say something quickly, but could not find the words. Jenny could see that Grace was struggling. "What the fuck?" Grace blurted out finally.

Jenny laughed out loud, abruptly unburdened, at least for the moment.

"It seems to me that you might have mentioned something like that. After all, we are investigating a mystery together."

Jenny continued. "Actually, I just found out."

"That's what you were doing in the restaurant?"

"Yeah. I already knew that I'd dealt a fairly substantial blow to some prick, but I didn't think I'd terminated him."

"Okay, let's hear the article."

Jenny read:

> *"The body of Chad Biswell, an itinerant farm worker, was found Saturday morning at Cornfield Cages batting range, by an employee. A police spokesman said that Biswell was killed by a blow to the head by a blunt instrument. A knife was found at the scene and it is not known if the knife was used in the apparent murder. The police say they have no leads other than a list of clients who used the range the night before the body was found. A source within the Police Department told the Tribune that Biswell had recently served time in a Nebraska prison for armed robbery."*

"I didn't hear your name in the article. What in the world is this all about? I'm looking for a possible murder victim with a murderer? You've got a little bit of explaining to do. I can't be involved with you, Jenny. Jesus, I thought you were helping me. Now I'm more scared than I was before we met."

"I'm really sorry. I guess I should have told you. That I'm telling you now, right after I first found out the guy died, should stand for something." Jenny looked over at Grace whose face looked like a sculpture. "The article was on page three. Doesn't that mean it wasn't significant? That nobody gives a shit about this creep?"

"Murder is murder, Sweetie. It doesn't matter who you kill. What kind of blunt instrument did you use."

"Duh. We were at a batting range, remember? It truly was a cases of self defense. That's why the knife was there. He held it to Kathy's neck. I took my shirt off and during the brief moment he was enjoying the view, I whacked him with a blunt instrument."

"Why didn't you call 911 right then?"

"Kathy wanted to, but if we'd done that, I'd probably be in Ames, Iowa until next summer."

"Jenny, you can't just make decisions like that. How many times have you heard someone say we have to live by the rules of society? Those are not just words. They are the obligations that assure that there's order in whatever social group we live in. What you did is exactly what your father would have done."

"Okay, here's the deal, Grace. I did the wrong thing. That toothpaste is already out of the tube. The water's out of the sink. It's done. What's done is done. It's not a knot that you can undo. Time to move on. We've got to find Roscoe Toth."

"Clever talk is not what I want out of you right now, Jenny. It's just a matter of time before the police come calling. It says in the article that they have the client list. Who signed in? You, or Kathy?"

"Neither one of us. I signed in as Amy Toth. That's who my fake license says I am. But this is the really haunting part – spooky – too coincidental. While we were in the Hi-Lo, I googled Amy Toth. Of course I expected to find no such person. But there is a person named Amy Toth on the entomology faculty at Iowa State. I'm sure you know it, but Iowa State is in Ames. So what am I supposed to do? Give Amy a call and tell her not to worry, that I did it? Obviously not. Grace, we've got to proceed as if none of this ever happened. I have to say this, though I feel really bad for the real Amy in Ames. I also googled Roscoe Toth while we were there. No such person."

"If you aren't on Google, it doesn't mean you don't exist."

Jenny was relieved that Grace was distracted. "Well, it's curious enough. Pretty much all it takes is having a phone."

"We're going to deal with Roscoe tomorrow. I can see that we're stuck with what you've done, but I'm not finished talking about it. I can't set my mind at ease until I know more details."

"Okay, I also googled the address that's on my fake I.D., 5210 Estates Drive, Atlanta. There is, indeed, such an address in Atlanta, and it happens to be for sale. Grace, I think the police in Ames will beat their brains out for awhile – they will certainly hassle poor Amy Toth in the entomology department, but it won't be too long before this gets relegated to the inactive file. When I signed in at the cages, I didn't have to put an address on the register, and the guy at the desk looked at the fake license for about two seconds."

"What about finger prints?"

"Grace, I love it. Now you're in the right frame of mind. First, we review the clue trail; second, we evaluate the probability of being found; third, if found, review the probability of being arrested. There were no finger prints. I thought about that, but I couldn't have left any because I was holding a bat in my left hand and signed in with my right. The pen had a great logo so I kept it. The only part of my hand that touched the sign-in sheet was the edge that rests on the paper when you write."

"What about Kathy?"

"She's home free, as long as she keeps her mouth shut. She never signed anything, and we left nothing behind that could ever link her to killing this creep. She just has to keep from telling her father, who is as straight as a laser. I'm going to have to call Kath and make sure she knows that."

"I wish you hadn't told me this, Jenny. It's weird though. I like the idea of full disclosure and honesty, but you've unwittingly made me an accomplice."

"Grace, the clue trail is non-existent. No worries."

"Okay. For now we'll leave it there. Keep in mind that you've given me some pretty good leverage. Don't get out of hand."

CHAPTER THIRTEEN

At Bend, they quickly decided to drive the remaining two and a half hours north to Dufur. After a stop at Taco Bell they were on the road again.

"Are you okay driving?" Jenny asked. "I have a license. A real one I mean, with my name on it. I've never driven a Prius, but I've watched you, and don't see you doing anything different."

"You're right. Pretty much like any other car. I'm doing fine for now."

Although their conversation had been intense, Jenny had been aware of the spectacular scenery as they drove through Bend. At least seven mountains, all completely blanketed with snow, were visible at once. It was still a bluebird day, and the mountains almost shimmered.

It was a huge relief to Jenny that they had finished, at least for the time being, the interrogation-like discussion about the Cornfield Cages Caper. It would have to come up again because Jenny needed to talk to Kathy soon, and she would have to summarize the substance of it to Grace. For now, it was behind them.

"How about we discuss a plan of action for when we get to Dufur?" Jenny inquired.

"Good idea. It will save us time tomorrow when we get started."

"Or tonight."

"I'm not seventeen, Jen. We can make a plan as we're driving, but we don't implement until tomorrow."

"By implement you mean spring into action right?"

"You know what I mean. You're starting to annoy me, Jenny."

"You're just mad because I'm a murderer."

"Drop it."

"Okay. So how do you envision the plan of our quest to find your old colleague, Roscoe? As I learned in Weed, there's no such person."

"I was thinking we should go to the police first."

"And do what? Remember I'm a murderer. We usually stay away from the police."

"God damn it, Jenny. Grow up."

"Grace, I'm really sorry. I'm wired. I can't seem to calm down."

"I understand that. Try to focus on the task at hand. Maybe the police station isn't the right place anyway. How about the public library or DHS?"

"What the hell is DHS?"

"The high school. Dufur High School."

"Of course. What would we do there?"

"If we assume that Roscoe attended Cal for four years and worked for two or three post-grad, he would have graduated from DHS six or seven years ago. We could try to get the Dufur High School year book from those years and look through the senior class pictures."

"That's brilliant. You'd make a good investigator."

"That's what I've been doing for the last four years. Just a different kind of investigation."

"So you think that the library or the high school is the best place to look for a year book?"

"It's a starting point. Have you got a better bet?"

"No. I lean toward the high school option. Probably the library there, wouldn't you think?"

"Yes. And what if we strike out?" Grace wondered.

"We can ask people, I guess. The problem is that since his name isn't Roscoe they won't know who we're talking about."

"I've been thinking that we need to ask around about the big wheat farmers in the area. One clue, if he was telling me the truth, is that the Roscoe family farm is one of the few irrigated ones. Maybe there's a rancher's supply store in town where we could get some information."

"That's a great idea, Grace. Even if we can find a photograph of Roscoe, we will still need to find out where the ranch is. So the sequence will be, one, the high school library; two, the ranch and feed supply store; and three, the wheat ranch. That's the part that might be scary."

℣

When they got to Dufur, they drove through the small downtown area and after a short discussion, decided that there might be some advantages to staying at the Balch Hotel. The cost of a double room was beyond what they had hoped to pay, but the exquisite historic landmark was a grand setting they could not resist. More important, it seemed to be a place where they could ask questions without raising suspicion.

In all her adult years, Grace had never gone into a bar alone. She knew, however, from watching television, that bar tenders know what's going on – at least in the bar. In a small town like Dufur, it seemed logical to presume that a bar tender would know as much or more about the local citizenry than anyone. Or maybe the barbershop. She imagined that would be a gossipy locale. Grace told Jenny all of this and said she was heading out to the bar and would be back in a half hour.

"I'll go with you."

"You're not old enough, Jen. Sorry. I'll have to handle this alone, I'm afraid."

"Um... Who's Jen? I'm Amy. See?" Jenny held her bogus license up.

"Get outta here. We're not going there, Sweetie."

"Come on. What's to worry about? The most they could do is kick me out?"

"Jennifer Lindsey, you are walking on thin ice. You stay here. I am going alone."

"Oh, yes, of course," Jenny sulked.

A few minutes after Grace left, Jenny went downstairs and asked the desk clerk about wheat farming. "Is it true that some growers have irrigation and some don't?"

"I believe that's the way it works. Wait here a moment."

Jenny was upset that she'd apparently been blown off by this guy, but she stood by the desk. When the clerk returned he said, "Come with me." He escorted her into the dining room where a man in Wrangler jeans and a western shirt sat at a side table with a bottle of Black Butte Pale Ale and a basket of hot wings. "This is Rocky Sherbine." The clerk then turned to Jenny. "And you are?"

"Jennifer Lindsey."

"Mr. Sherbine is a wheat rancher east of here. He said he'd be happy to talk to you."

"Hi, Jennifer," said Sherbine. "What can I do for you?" Sherbine's voice was deep and slow.

"I'm doing a term paper on wheat ranching and right now I'm discussing irrigation, water rights, stuff like that. I just wanted to get some first hand info."

"Mine's all dry land stuff. There's a few down closer to the river that have irrigation. They get a little more production, but I like it up here on higher ground. We do okay."

"So if I wanted to check out one of the irrigated farms, I'd go down toward the river?"

"Yeah. Yeah, that's what you'd do."

"What river is it?"

"The Columbia. The Columbia River. That's the river."

"Of course. I don't know what I was thinking."

"Just go north on the highway, toward The Dalles, and you might see the irrigation equipment on some of the places before you get there. There's one or two off to the east."

"Do you know Roscoe Toth?"

"No. Can't say that I do. There was a Toth here in Wasco County, but I'm pretty sure it wasn't Roscoe. About ten years ago, the guy up and disappeared. I kind of liked the little man. He was always up to some scheme, but he was pretty cheerful, and I liked him. My wife, Terri, would probably know more about his disappearance and some of the investigations that went on back then."

"That's very interesting, but I guess I won't need it for my term paper." Jenny wanted to know more about what the rumors might be, but didn't think her term paper story would hold up if she diverted attention to that. "Who has the biggest irrigated wheat farm up that way?"

"Well, let me think." Sherbine picked up the amber bottle and took a slow gulp. "I'm not sure, Jenny. I guess it might be Larry Jepson. He's probably got the biggest spread. He's up north-east of here not too far from the river. Another guy is Dan Parker, but I think Jepson's place is producing more wheat. They're both pretty good guys, and might be willing to talk to you a little bit about water and wheat. As I said, I grow the dry land kind. It makes things a little less complex."

"Thanks, Rocky. I've got to go back to my room and write this stuff down before I forget. You said, Jepson and Parker?"

"Yeah those are the big ones. By the way, Larry's married to the former Margo Toth. She used to be married to the guy who disappeared. I'll tell you what. If you can't get what you need from either of those guys, come to my place tomorrow and talk to my wife. She knows the business as well as I do and she'd be happy to talk to you about water. Here's our number. He handed her a business card."

"You're a peach, Mr. Sherbine. Thanks."

"Can't say as I've ever been called a peach before, but you're welcome."

Jenny hurried up to their room and made notes on the names and directions that Rocky had given her.

Not long after she finished, Grace keyed the door and came in looking a little discouraged. "Well, that was a wild goose chase," she said.

"Why do you say that?"

"The only place I found close by was sort of a saloon. There were a bunch of Harleys parked outside, but I braved it and went in anyway. It was scary. I clinched my teeth and went up to the bar to ask for a draft and the bartender pointed to an array of handles. I didn't know what he wanted so I stood there for awhile. Finally he shrugged his shoulders and walked away. There was a guy standing next me, and he told me that the barkeep – that's what he called him – wanted me to choose a brand. Eventually the bartender – I prefer that word – came back and stood there, so I said Coors Light. Luckily they had it. I don't know where I would have gone next. But anyway, the bartender had been so sullen about taking my order that I drank half my beer as fast as I could and got out of there."

As Jenny listened to Grace's story, she began to gloat, anxious to say how much she had learned in a short time downstairs in their own hotel. But suddenly a sense of compassion came over her. *This wonderfully successful woman had to suffer through an indignity that would have caused me to cry, and maybe lie about it, and she just walked out of the place and told me the whole story.* At that moment Jenny decided it was essential that she take care in her response. This was an opportunity to either build trust – maybe even admiration – or add to the failure and disgrace that Grace was already feeling.

"Was the place full of bikers?" Jenny asked.

"It looked like everyone in there was a biker. The guy standing next to me looked like Methuselah with a leather vest and leather pants. But I'll say this about him. He was nice enough. I couldn't tell whether they were locals or what, but they were from a world that I know nothing about, and I guess I'm scared of."

"I admire you, Grace."

"I got nothing. No matter we can go ahead with our plan tomorrow."

"Grace, almost accidentally I fell into some information that might turn out to be helpful."

Grace seemed cheered by the comment. "How?"

"Well, I was cold and couldn't figure out how to work the heater, so I went down to the lobby and asked at the desk how to get the room a little warmer. The guy told me there was a thermostat." Jenny pointed toward it as she spoke. "On a lark I just asked him if he knew anything about wheat farming and he was kind enough to introduce me to one of the local ranchers." From there, Jenny recounted the story as accurately as she could remember it.

"That's wonderful," Grace said.

CHAPTER FOURTEEN

The following morning – Monday – Jenny made a task list. It consisted of three items: 1) Call Kathy; 2) Find a high school yearbook; and 3) Go to Jepson ranch and talk to Larry or Margo Jepson. Jenny's feelings about calling Kathy were mixed. She looked forward to talking to her new friend, but she feared that Kathy might have buckled under the burden of keeping their secret and mentioned it to someone. She especially feared that she might have mentioned it to her laser-straight father. By time-zone, she was an hour behind Kathy, so she knew that it wouldn't be too early to call at 8:30. She had 78 minutes left on her prepaid cell, which would be more than ample.

When Kathy answered, Jenny said, "Hey, it's your partner in crime."

"Oh my god, I'm soooo glad you called. I'm dying."

"Don't die. I think we're good. I've gone over and over this thing, and I don't see any way that anyone can ever connect us. The only way, and this is my huge worry, is if anyone in your sorority knew we went over to the cages that night and put it together when they read it in the paper or saw it on TV."

"Okay, the good news is I didn't tell Dad. The bad news is that Beth, our chubby know-it-all did ask me about it. I had already thought of the possibility, and so I was quick with the answer that we'd gone bowling instead. I feigned great relief that we hadn't gone to the cages. She seemed satisfied, and even commented that we were really lucky. She remembered that she'd warned us and that I had agreed that maybe we shouldn't go. She even said, 'Seeeee?' I thanked her for the life-saving advice."

"It sounds like you covered the bases," Jenny said. "Nice work."

The two friends talked for fifteen minutes or so and finally Jenny had to say that she was on a mission and needed to ring off. Kathy said there was a chance that she and her father would fly out to California next summer. Jenny was pumped.

"Sounds like that is resolved," Grace said.

"I think we're good," Jenny repeated with an exaggerated sigh.

"So we can proceed to step two – find a six-year-old high school yearbook. I could be off by a couple years. We'll just have to see."

First they had breakfast in the Hotel dining room. While there they got directions to the high school. By the time they had repacked their overnight bags and checked out of the hotel it was 11:00. Shortly thereafter they were in the principal's office at Dufur High School. The principal, Lou Ferry, told them that the library would probably have a full set of Crimson and Whites. He gave them a library pass, and they excitedly proceeded to the school library. There was a student on duty at the check-out desk and she was cooperative in showing Grace and Jenny where the Crimson and Whites were. "Aren't you a student here?" she asked Jenny.

Jenny shook her head. "Nope."

They each took two volumes, figuring the four years they had would surely cover Roscoe's senior year. Jenny didn't know what Roscoe Toth looked like, so she just searched the alphabetically arrange photos for Toth. Neither of her volumes had a Toth. Grace did the same with the same result. The classes were not large, however, so it was not a major chore to look at the senior pictures page by page. Grace found Roscoe's photo in the third book she perused. She looked over at Jenny and pointed. "This is the guy. This is Roscoe Toth. I can't believe it was this easy."

"What's his real name?"

"Ross Jepson."

"How about that? So he really is from Dufur. Jepson. Okay. Remember I told you that Larry Jepson was the biggest wheat rancher? Well, Rocky also told me that Larry was married to the former Margo Toth. I looks kind of like Roscoe might be Margo's son."

"It sure does. The plot thickens."

CHAPTER FIFTEEN

Jenny and Grace thanked the student librarian, and returned to Lou Ferry's office. They thanked him, belatedly introduced themselves, and asked him if he knew where the Jepson property was. Ferry gave them explicit directions. "Mrs. Jepson's son was a student of ours. Excellent student. He went on to the University of California, I believe."

"You say Mrs. Jepson's son?"

"Mrs. Jepson's first husband was named Giuseppe Toth. He disappeared ten years ago or so, and she remarried about six years after that. The so called *Death in Absentia* law in Oregon is five years. That means if, for five years there is no evidence that a person is alive, he is presumed to be dead. The timing of Jepson's marriage to Ms. Toth raised not only eyebrows, but suspicions. I don't think Larry Jepson ever adopted Ross, but about the time he was a junior, or maybe not until he was a senior, Ross changed his name to Jepson anyway. The Jepson family has been producing wheat in this area for years – generations, I should say. At the time of his disappearance, Giuseppe was suspected in a number of different schemes in this small town. He was tried for selling mislabeled wine, but was acquitted. The wine scam was very simplistic. He would collect empty bottles and corks from expensive vineyards, fill them with similar tasting but less expensive wine and sell it through an on-line auction site."

Jenny found the information intriguing. "How did he get the bottles?" she asked.

"He scavenged them from restaurants. He would drive a van to Portland or Seattle and come back with cases of discarded bottles from upscale restaurants. There were some people here in Wasco County who didn't like him; but most did. He was something of a cult hero, you might say. For example, in spite of his small stature – I'd guess he was only about five-foot-four or so in boots – he was a member of the local bikers' club. In fact during the wine-scam trial, the courtroom was filled with members of his club, The Free Souls "

"Sounds like an interesting fellow," Grace offered.

"Giuseppe and Roscoe never got along, and I'm pretty sure that's why Ross took on Jepson's name even though he wasn't adopted."

"Kids do things for unknown reasons," Grace said.

Lou Ferry was enjoying this exchange. He had always been curious about the Toth family and the rumors that swirled around about Giuseppe's disappearance, and besides, he thought Grace was attractive. "Somehow your interest in Ross doesn't surprise me."

"Thank you Mr. Ferry," Jenny said. "We should probably head out to the Jepson's ranch."

"You don't need to be in a rush," Ferry said.

"No, we don't." agreed Grace.

Ferry went on. "Toth's disappearance was assumed to be murder. But the case was never resolved – that is, no arrest was ever made."

"Where did the suspicion focus?" Grace asked.

"Giuseppe, who always called himself Joe – was prominent in the respect that he was a visible part of the community. He was either at the grocery store, the bar where he worked, or the cafe every day. So when he suddenly was not seen for a day or two the police immediately assumed there was something amiss. The investigation was pretty well publicized in this small community, of course. Nobody was ever arrested.

Mrs. Jepson was actually one of the suspects. So was Ross, the son. There was also one other suspect. As I remember, the police had little doubt that Joe had been murdered, but they never could figure out who did it."

"This has been a most useful interview, Mr. Ferry," Grace said. "Ross Jepson, or Toth, as the case may be, told me that he had received a threatening phone call. He then disappeared. It almost sounds like a rerun of his father's life. I hope he hasn't been murdered. We're trying to find out if he's hiding because of the calls, or just what's going on. I expect that the first thing we do will be to go down to the Jepson place and talk to Mr. and Mrs. Jepson."

"Mr. Jepson is a forthright citizen — not endowed with social skills by any stretch — but a nice enough guy. To be fair, I should say that Mrs. Jepson — Margo, I believe her name is — is reasonably well regarded except for the uncertainty surrounding her role in the disappearance of Toth. If you want to find out anything about Mrs. Jepson's past, be very tactful. She gets defensive about that in a hurry. If you have time, I'd like to hear what you find out. I'd like to take you and your daughter to dinner if you'd care to join me."

Grace liked Ferry's manner, but as she mulled the implications and possible delays in their time line, Jenny spoke up. "I'm not Grace's daughter, Mr. Ferry. I'm her friend."

"Well, I apologize. The invitation stands."

"It's kind of you, Mr. Ferry, but we're pressed for time, so I think we must decline. If I might have your cell number I could call and tell you what we learn. It might even turn out that we will have more questions."

Ferry gave Grace his number, and Grace and Jenny left the principal's office with a map to the Jepson place that Ferry had drawn for them. When they got to the car, Jenny said, "I don't think we should go directly out there."

"For goodness sake, why not?"

"When I was telling you about my conversation with Rocky, I forgot to mention that he had told me about Toth's mysterious disappearance. He said he didn't know much, but thought his wife might. I'm just thinking it might help us with our interview if we know as much as we can about Mrs. Jepson's background."

"Jenny, sometimes you surprise me. That's pretty good thinking. After all, Roscoe was raised by her. She'd be the one who shaped who he is now. She and the late Giuseppe Toth. It's possible that his disappearance and the Roscoe Toth disappearance don't have anything to do with each other, but the more information we go in with, the better we will be able to determine the truthfulness of what we're being told."

"So we go to the Sherbines'? Maybe we should call first. He gave me a business card."

Grace's call was answered by Mrs. Sherbine, who invited them to come out to their place. The drive took fifteen minutes or so, and when they arrived, Jenny was reminded of her visit to the Belton farm. There were multiple buildings and an array of equipment that would take someone in the business to know what it was for. Terri Sherbine was sitting in a swing on the front porch. After introductions, she invited them inside the elegantly decorated farmhouse.

Jenny opened with an apology. "When I met Rocky, I didn't know how to ask for the information I wanted so I made up a story that I was writing a term paper. Truth be told, I'm not."

"He didn't tell me that anyway. Why don't you tell me what you want?"

"This is really Grace's situation," Jenny said, looking toward her friend.

Grace explained why they were looking for the man she knew as Roscoe Toth and that she and Jenny had discovered that in High School Roscoe had called himself Ross Jepson. Although Grace felt an immediate comfort and trust in Terri,

93

she left out certain details of the story. She didn't mention the death threat, for example, nor her fear that she might be next. She also was not fully disclosing about her research, only saying that she was developing new pesticides. Terri mentioned that farming involved a constant battle with pests and wished Grace success.

Terri went on to tell them that she had become acquainted with Margo through a ranchers' wives group, but had never got to know her well, because Terri was so busy with the business aspects of their own farm that she seldom went to meetings. Terri repeated the stories that they had heard from Lou Ferry about the fraudulent schemes that Giuseppe Toth had come up with to make money.

"Joe made his legal money as a bartender. In fact the first anybody ever knew of him he had been hired by Cindy Wilson who owned the local tavern. Joe was always cheerful and right away became something of a local hero because of his antics behind the bar. Terry didn't know exactly what he did, but he was the talk of the town for awhile. It was well known around town that there were things about Joe that Cindy Wilson didn't like. But he was bringing in customers, so she put up with him.

"Everybody was surprised when, following the declared death of Joe Toth, Margo married Jepson. Jepson was 40 years old and had never married. It was widely believed that he never would – that he was wedded to his wheat farming and the innovative growing and harvesting techniques that he had developed. The gossip about why this decent, albeit somewhat strange, man had married Margo was viral. The consensus was the Margo somehow got this man into a sexual relationship and showed him some possibilities that theretofore were unknown to the asexual loner. The marriage put Margo into the society scene, such as it is in Dufur, and she thrived on it – at least her ego did. She never got over her roving eye, but as far as Terri knew, she had not been caught being unfaithful.

"Roscoe appeared to get along with Jepson, but there were some of Joe's traits in him, too." By that Terri explained that she meant that he was a constant discipline problem during his years in school. Nevertheless, he was without question, the smartest kid in his class, and he did not hesitate to make people aware of that fact.

"Did Rocky tell you anything about Giuseppe Toth's disappearance?"

"No," Jenny said. "I just wanted to find out who the big wheat ranchers were up here. So that's all Rocky and I talked about."

"Let me bring you some tea and then I'll tell you what I know," Terri said. She returned with three mugs of tea and a plate of almond cookies, sat down and continued.

"Giuseppe closed up his boss's bar at 1:30 on a Tuesday, I think. He often did not return home to the trailer where his wife and son lived outside of town. The waitress at the diner where he often had breakfast noticed that he did not show up the next morning, and then he missed his four o'clock shift at the bar. There was no suicide note. Margo said that he did not come home after his shift, but that it was not unusual for him to do that. I think the cops suspected foul play from the very outset, but they could never find the body. Moreover, they found no clues that would lead them to a suspect. At least that's what they told the public. You never know if you're getting the whole story from the cops, of course. They had very few details.

"Some of Roscoe's friends told the police that Roscoe did not like his father, but others said he talked about him as a 'cool dude who knew how to play the system.' Both Roscoe and Margo had motives, and then there was one member of the biker club that they were looking at. Can't remember what the deal on him was, but we knew the guy, and we never thought that murder would be this man's solution to anything. Besides it was pretty well known that Joe Toth was something of a club icon in The Free Souls."

"What were the motives?" Grace inquired.

"We're pretty sure that Roscoe really did not like Giuseppe. And of course as it turned out, Margo freed herself up to marry one of the richest men in Wasco County."

Jenny spoke up. "And at the time that couldn't have been known as a motive."

"Good point, Jenny. That's about it. None of this really sheds any light on what you guys are trying to find out, but I hope it gives you a sense of guidance on how to talk to the Jepsons. I guess it doesn't matter which one you talk to, but I can say with certainty that Larry is the one that will give you straight answers without any innuendo. But you have to be pretty forthcoming with the guy. He'll let you know if he thinks you're being too sneaky. By the way, he never was real fond of Ross."

Terri stood and offered more tea, which was politely refused. "I've got wine or beer."

The women smiled and said no. "Well then, how about coming back after you talk to them. Rocky would want to know what you find out. We can have the wine and beer then."

CHAPTER SIXTEEN

It appeared that the Jepson ranch had been plowed and perhaps seeded. It was a picture of organization, with all the vehicles parked in a pattern that evoked a farm magazine cover. In spite of the winter season, center pivot irrigation systems were raining water on the farmland, and a couple of substantial ponds were visible at an elevation below where the women stopped in the driveway. A new warehouse sized building was under construction not far from the pond, and the Columbia River was beyond – perhaps a half mile away.

A hefty man in a baseball cap and open necked shirt strode toward them with a half smile. "Help ya?" he said.

Grace found Larry's size and demeanor intimidating. "Are you Mr. Jepson?"

"Larry Jepson."

"My name is Grace Summers and this is my friend Jennifer Lindsey. I think it's possible that your son worked for me."

"Possible, I guess."

"Do you talk to him on a regular basis?"

"Yep. Yep, fairly regular, I guess. Every week or so. Sometimes it'll run out to two or three."

"Did he tell you what his job was?"

"Yep. He sure did."

"What did he say he was doing?"

"Well if he worked for you it seems like you should know what he was doin'."

97

"Well, of course I know what the guy who worked for me did. I'm trying to find out if it was your son who worked for me."

"Well, what was the guy's name? The one who worked for you."

"It was Roscoe. Roscoe Toth."

"Sounds like him all right. He used that name sometimes."

"Well he used it the whole time he was at the university. He also used it the whole time he worked for me."

"M'self – I never liked his usin' that name. I'm not his real dad. His real dad was a guy named Toth, and I never liked the guy. Never liked the name, but I don't know if it's because of the way the name sounds when you say it, or whether it's because I didn't like the guy whose name it was."

"I'm just trying to verify that your son is who worked for me."

"Can't be much doubt about that. He worked at a bug plant down in California. That's about all I ever knew. Is that all you wanted?"

"Well, no, Mr. Jepson… "

"Why don't you just call me Larry?"

"Okay, well he didn't show up for work for over a week, and I was worried."

"Worried?"

"Yes, I was worried."

"Well, Lady… "

"Why don't you just call me Grace?"

"Okay, well I don't think you have much to worry about."

"Why in the world would you say that?"

"Because I don't think there is. Anything to worry about, I mean."

"Have you heard from him?"

"As I said, he calls up every so often."

"Have you talked to him In the last week?"

"Nope."

"Doesn't that worry you?"

"Nope. His calls are not like clock work. He calls every week or two. I'm not worried because nobody but you has told me anything that should worry me. I gather you think I should worry."

"Of course I do. Why in the world do you think we're here?"

"I thought it was to find out if it's Ross that works for you."

"Well, yes. I wanted to make sure I was at the right place before I worried you that Ross is missing."

"Is he missing, or did he just miss work? There's real difference."

"Larry," Graced felt herself grimace as she said his name, "Roscoe told me that he had received a threatening call from a pesticide manufacturing company."

"Well why didn't you tell me that in the first place? What one?"

"I don't know. He didn't tell me."

"Did you ask him?"

"I don't know. I don't know, uh.. Larry. I just don't remember."

Jenny had been silent during this interview and could not stand the way it was going. To her it was like a boxing match with a lot of bobbing and weaving, but no punches. "Listen Larry," she said at long last, "we came up here from Berkeley in one day. It was a long trip, but we did it because Roscoe got a death threat from a pesticide company, and we thought you should know about it. He did not give Grace many details, and Grace assumes it's because whoever threatened him didn't give him many. My guess is that's standard with death threats. Minimal details.

"Your son knows how to make some very sophisticated pesticides and the company that threatened Roscoe wants to find out what he knows. Failing that, they would kill him – at least that's what he said they told him. Obviously, the com-

99

pany hired whoever made the call, but it seems to me that the managers of this company are trying to prevent Roscoe from making products that could hurt their company's sales. Now, that's all Grace knows at this point, but she is worried about your son, and it seems logical to me that you might be also."

"Well, now that you put it that way, I guess I am a little worried. But I'll tell you this. Even though he's smart and can be a good worker, he's also a pain in the ass. Ever since I knew him he would just about convince you he was reliable and then he'd disappoint. So if I was to make a guess right here, it'd be that he ain't killed. In fact, I figure he's going to show up here, and after what you say, I think it will be within a week or two.

"I knew that he had some kind of research job. He never said much about it. But the way he spoke about it, it wasn't going to be his life. Three or four years ago when he finished college he came up here talking about using our water to grow wild rice. For awhile he was interested in fish. He visited two or three hatcheries. One of em's downstream from here at Bonneville Dam; but in the end, he thought wild rice was the way to go. I've got a right to more water than I need, and I have to use it or they take it away. I get a little more production than the dry-land guy up the hill, but not that much more. Maybe not even enough more than he does to pay for all the water I use. So this kid we're talking about, the Toth boy, he has this idea to grow wild rice. That's his latest brainchild anyhow.

"You probably know that for years all the wild rice came out of Minnesota. It really did grow wild and was harvested by the Indians up there – the Chippewas, I think. Then somebody figured out that the reason it was wild up there and grew so well was the combination of the water and the weather. You have to freeze the seed for a certain amount of time or it won't germinate. That's what that building right down there is for. It's a freezer building. Maybe they germinate the seed in there, too. I don't know."

Grace was speechless. None of what Larry had said fit her expectations of what Roscoe would do or even think about. As she thought about it now, she realized that she never heard him talk about his future. Finally she said, "This all comes as quite a surprise, Larry."

"Well, it's just to say there's probably nothing to worry about. Roscoe marches to a different drum. Probably more accurate to say he hears the same drum we all do, but he makes a choice to stay out of time with it."

Larry ran his fingers though his hair, frowned a bit, and looked Grace squarely in the eye. "By the way, your friend Jenny there knows how to ask a question. I didn't know what in the hell you were trying to find out. I even thought you might be undercover cops. They sniff around here now and then because they can't figure out who killed old man Toth, that pile of shit. Anything else?"

Grace reviewed the conversation and couldn't think of anything more to ask. She handed Larry a business card and asked him if he would kindly call when he heard from Roscoe. "Roscoe was a big help to me. He is a quick learner and knows how to apply what he learns. I sometimes had to remind him that he was supposed to stick to certain tasks, and usually he did. I hope you're right and that he's okay. Let me know – please."

As they turned to walk to their car, Larry walked along with them. "Sure. I'll give you a call."

During the discussion, Jenny had been watching a D-8 pushing earth around on the downside of the new building. "Does your property go all the way down to the river?" she asked.

"Right there it does. Not to the Columbia, but to the Deschutes. The Deschutes flows into the Columbia about a mile downriver from my property. By that I mean I have about a quarter mile frontage on the Deschutes about a mile upstream from its mouth on the Columbia. It's like a finger of land we own. That there thing that they're building is going to be an effluent flume. He's got some way of treating the water before it discharges into the river. It's all got permits and all that bullshit that they make us do these days."

"Thanks again," Grace said. "Good luck."

"I'll tell you something you don't need to know, Grace." He looked at Jenny. "You, too. I don't like what he's doing. At first it seemed like a real project. But now I'm not sure. He keeps changing things for no apparent reason. I have to let him do it to keep Margo happy. All right, that's it. I don't know where he is, but he has showed up here at least once a month, even when he was at the university, so if somebody offs him, I won't even notice it for awhile."

CHAPTER SEVENTEEN

Larry stood beside the silver Prius as the women got in. He still wore a smirky smile that made Grace think there was something behind it. She wondered if she was making something out of nothing. She looked at Jenny who had her usual bright look as she gazed about the wheat ranch. "Well," Grace said, after they were underway, "What did you think of that?"

"I have to say, it shakes me up a little that they're still sniffing around about Giuseppe Toth's murder after all these years. I thought that the cops had some kind of a timetable that clicks off the investigation at some point."

"I can see why you might focus on that. But I was wondering what you thought about the interview."

"Well, as you might have noticed, I didn't like the sparring match at the beginning, but all in all, I would have to think you are relieved. I couldn't figure out why you didn't just give him the facts right off the bat. I think he got defensive the way you were talking to him."

"I'm inclined to agree with you, Jenny. I didn't do very well. Thank you for bailing me out."

Jenny took a folded paper out of her back pocket and opened it up. "We really haven't learned anything for sure." She looked at the outline that she had made driving back from Reno. "Right now, I'm leaning toward III. B. That's the one where the assumption is that Roscoe did not get any call and made up the story. It's also the place in the outline I didn't know how to identify choices, so I put question marks. The thing is, we don't know for sure. The poor guy might be tied to a stretcher in somebody's basement, for all we know. It just seems like what we've heard about his background makes it not unlikely – my dad used to say 'not unlikely' all the time – that he would make up a story like that. As Larry implied, he's out of step, knows it, and chooses to stay that way."

"You are very analytical, Jenny. Maybe I should offer you a job."

"I think you did that in Reno, didn't you? Therapist, as I re-call."

"That was a swap, my friend. Remember you got a ride out of the deal."

"Pretty exciting ride, so far. What do we do next. I've got about two weeks to go before registration."

"We're sure as hell not going to last two weeks on our bud-get. Still, even though it looks less likely that Roscoe has been snuffed, I'd like to learn as much as we can about why he just up and left without any warning. As you told Larry, it was a long trip. I hope we don't have to make it again."

"I think we should stop by Rocky and Terri's place before we take off. It's only 2:30, so we would have time to do something else first if we want."

"I wish we'd asked Larry who was telling the excavation contractors what to do, Jenny. Larry acted like it was Roscoe's project, but Roscoe is nowhere around."

"I've been thinking the same thing. All the time we were talking with Larry, I had the feeling that there was something that was being left unsaid. Some kind of secret agenda. But I can't figure out anything it could be. It doesn't quite fit that if he dislikes Roscoe as much as he pretends to, that he would spend the kind of money it must be costing him to support what he called Roscoe's brainchild. He said it like he thought is was a harebrained scheme."

"I'm also wondering if we should have talked to Margo Jepson. When we got there, I was glad that it was Larry who greeted us, but we might have learned something from Margo if we'd talked to her. One thing is certain. Margo and Roscoe are a couple of paupers who now find themselves in opulence."

"I wonder who winds up with this property if Jepson buys the farm," added Jenny.

∞

Two people watched through the window as Jenny and Grace talked to Larry Jepson. "Do you know who them two are that's talkin' to Larry?"

"I know who one of em is. She's – or maybe I should say she was – my boss down in Berkeley. She's smart. Not someone to ignore."

"What do you mean by 'not someone to ignore'?"

"Mother, what part of that simple statement do you not understand?"

"Screw you, Rosco. You'd better get back to your cabin. Lawrence will be coming in pretty soon."

∞

When the Prius got to the junction at Highway 197, Grace asked, "Back to Dufur, or to the Sherbines'?"

"Let's make a quick trip to Bonneville Dam."

"There's a surprise."

"Jepson said Roscoe had visited the hatchery there. Let's see if we can find out what might have interested him."

They turned north and merged onto I-84 at The Dalles. The route westward to the dam was clearly marked and after some 50 miles along the interstate, they took the driveway into the visitor's center. There they found an inviting gallery with many free pamphlets extolling the virtues of this Corps of Engineers project. A uniformed young man pointed them to the hatchery viewing area. After a short walk they were greeted by another uniform who told them a little about the facility and pointed to more leaflets.

Jenny asked the man how long he'd worked there.

"A little over a year," said the man whose name tag carried the name *Don*. Jenny immediately surmised from the number of people wandering around the facility, that even if Don had been there three years ago, he could never have remembered a certain guy, even if they had a photograph of him. "Do you put the fish into the river?" she asked.

"Yes. The fish we release supplement the natural spawning production. These pamphlets explain the whole process, from egg to release. If you want, you can check out the upstream migrants through the viewing window and walk around the raceways. Feel free to wander around and ask any questions that come to mind."

"Thanks," Jenny and Grace said in unison.

They looked at each other and without saying a word, headed back to where they had left the Prius. When they got to the car, Grace said, "We can probably learn more online than we can from these pamphlets. I have to say, it's a pretty remarkable place."

"Mike, the truck driver who picked me up, told me some stuff about hatcheries. His dad told him that hatchery- produced salmon were weakening the gene pool of the wild populations. He didn't really understand the situation, so naturally I didn't either, but I'll bet there's some info about that online, as well. I doubt the Corps of Engineers mentions anything about that in their pamphlet."

CHAPTER EIGHTEEN

By the time they got back to The Dalles it was 5:00. Both women felt like the trip to the hatchery had added nothing to the information pool they were trying to fill. "I wonder if it's too late to visit Rocky and Terri," Jenny said.

"Well, we have their number. Let's call and ask." Jenny made the call with Grace's phone and Terri encouraged them to drop by.

When they arrived, Terri invited them into a heated greenhouse, where Rocky sat near a gas fire ring sipping a Coors Light. "Hello, Jenny," he said. "Did you get a chance to talk to any of those guys?"

On a table at the side of the greenhouse stood a couple bottles of wine, several more Coors, and an array of cheeses, dry salamis and crackers. Jenny introduced Grace to Rocky and told him that they had met and talked to Larry Jepson. "Kind of a weirdo, if you ask me," Jenny said.

"He's a pretty good farmer, Jenny," Rocky said in a way that imparted the information but did not sound critical of Jenny's remark.

"Good farmer, strange man."

Grace added, "Jenny told me about the conversation she had with you at the hotel last night. She left out some of the details of why we came up here. At the time we just wanted to find the guy who turned out to be Jepson because I knew from having known Roscoe for a few years that his family had an irrigated wheat farm near Dufur. This morning we filled Terri in on more of the details of why we came up here, but the main one I left out was that before he disappeared, Roscoe told me that he'd received a death threat."

"Did whoever threatened him want him to do something, or maybe not do something, Jenny?"

"Yes. Somehow they thought he was the guy who knew how to make certain pesticides that whoever it was that made the call thought would put a company – he didn't say what one – out of business. Right after that, Roscoe disappeared."

"And Ross was working for you, Grace?"

"Yes. He ran some analytical equipment I had in my lab."

"I'm surprised you came all the way up here because of that. Why don't you just hire a new guy?"

"I could do that. The reason I'm worried is that if the call was really made and the reason that Roscoe is missing is that he was murdered, then I could be next. It's really me and not Roscoe that knows how to make these specific pesticides."

"What do you want me to do, Grace?"

"Nothing. I just wanted to thank you for pointing us in the right direction to find Jepson. We learned quite a bit by talking to him. Call this a social visit."

"Well, if I see Ross around, should I give you a call?"

"That would be great. Same with Terri. Jenny and I have the same hunch that Roscoe made up the threat story, but we can't be sure. So if either of you should see him or hear that he's around, I would really appreciate a call." Grace gave Rocky a card with her number.

"Okay, Grace, we sure will."

Jenny and Grace stayed for a couple of hours more eating and drinking the generous offerings of the Sherbines. Rocky had known Larry Jepson for years although they seldom saw each other and had never done business together. He knew that Jepson was interested in using his water to better advantage, but hadn't ever come up with any ideas of how to use it.

By the time they left, Jenny and Grace knew that they would have to spend another night in Dufur. "What if you live in Dufur?" Jenny remarked. "What would you ever do?"

"It would be a challenge," replied Grace.

"Maybe we should go into your favorite bar and ask about Joe Toth. He used to work there after all."

"Good plan, Jenny. You do that and I'll wait for you at the hotel."

"No. Just sayin', there's probably a bunch of guys in there who were friends with him. It would be cool to find out what this guy was really like. If nothing else, he sounds intriguing."

"Let's not lose sight of what we came here for. We wanted to learn about Roscoe. I don't think we're going to learn any more. I'd say we did very well for a couple outsiders in a tight little community like Dufur. My thought is that we won't get any more puzzle pieces, but if we give it some thought, we might be able to further interpret what we've heard."

"For example?"

"Well, Jenny, we both think that Roscoe is alive, and that he made up the story about the threat call. Why? What did we learn that really supports that?"

"First I want to say *nothing*. It's just intuition. But you're correct that we should try to reason out why we both feel that way."

"It came out of the Larry Jepson conversation, Jenny. Larry wasn't the least bit worried, so we conclude Larry must be right and the whole Roscoe murder/disappearance deal is bogus. Pretty thin evidence."

"So, what? We're going to head back and say, 'mission not accomplished'? We have to believe our feeling."

"I don't know where to go from here. Back to the police in Richmond? Maybe we should talk to the police in Dufur."

"Bingo. Dufur police. After all they already have one missing Toth. Might as well make it two. It'll be a two-fer in Dufur."

CHAPTER NINETEEN

The two women considered changing to less expensive lodging, but discovered that they would have to go back to The Dalles in order to do so. The next morning, they ate a light breakfast at the Balch Hotel and proceeded to the Dufur City Hall. Upon asking directions to the police office they were told that Dufur's police services were provided by The Dalles police and the Wasco County sheriff, both located in The Dalles.

"I guess we should have spent the night there after all," Jenny remarked.

"I don't know if we should even take the time to go there. It's a long way back to Berkeley and even if we head straight south, it will be well after dark before we get there."

"I'll help you drive if you get tired."

"I might let you this time. Let's go talk to the police."

When they arrived at the police station they were shown into the office of Sergeant Lem Russell by a prim woman with dyed black hair, purple lipstick and mascara, and glitter nail polish. Lem listened to the story that Grace related and said that he had been involved in the missing person investigation of Giuseppe Toth.

"If Ross is truly missing, it must be some kind of record – two Toths disappear separately in a small town like Dufur," Lem speculated.

"I don't know about that. I just think you should be on the lookout for Roscoe, or Ross Jepson, if that's what he's called up here."

"That was a weird case – the Joe Toth deal. He was as regular as the tides about his life-style. Never missed work, rarely missed breakfast at the diner, and always answered his cell phone. Mrs. Toth told me that even if he didn't return home after work that he always went home after his meal at the diner. When Ms. Toth phoned us mid-morning after he didn't go back home after work, I figured he'd crashed on that long winding road into his place. I drove out there and there was no sign of any such thing. Right then I said to myself, 'the old lady did it.' Probably unprofessional for me to tell you that, but it's something that I just thought. Thing is we never could find any evidence that he was dead. Some folks up in Dufur who knew him well figured he up and left, changed his name and started a new life somewhere. All kinds of stories started getting made up about what he might be doing and where he might be doing it.

"Now you tell me the son is missing, too. That makes me wonder if what some of these folks think, might just be true. Maybe Joe got in touch with Ross, and they're bagging rays on the beach at Acapulco. One thing though – Ross had a pretty good deal going here. Larry Jepson treated that kid pretty damn well. I get the idea that he don't like the kid all that much, but Larry's a good guy, and he takes good care of the kid. Sent him to college; buys him pretty much everything the kid needs. I don't know. That old boy Jepson is a kind soul. I can't really see Joe running away from what he has here."

Grace found the new idea that Roscoe might be somewhere with Giuseppe Toth intriguing. But she had never heard Roscoe talk about his family at all – only the wheat farm in Dufur. It seemed to her a very remote possibility that Roscoe would do something like that. So far, no useful information.

"What can you tell me about the investigation itself? I'm talking about the father's disappearance. Were there search parties sent out looking for him or for his body?"

"Yep, there sure were. We had a hundred volunteers, at least. We probably scoured 20 square miles. Dogs. The whole Maryanne. There was a lot of people up in Dufur who really loved that man. You know a bartender is a guy you spill out yer guts to. He's like an untrained therapist."

That remark caused Grace to think of her short acquaintance with Jenny. Jenny had actually been very helpful in settling her down and enabling her to organize her thinking about Roscoe.

"Can I file a missing person report on Roscoe?"

"Nope. He ain't missing up here. He's missing in Berkeley from what you told me."

"I just thought that since he's from Dufur this is where he might go to if he isn't dead. Then he'd be missing locally."

"I'll just write up our conversation and put it in our computer files. Some IT guy came in here a few years back and got us up to speed on all our electronic systems. We're probably as good as the FBI. If anything remotely connected to Ross Jepson or Roscoe Toth comes up, we will automatically find the file of our conversation and it will help us."

"You haven't looked at your computer since we got here," Jenny pointed out.

"Don't need to with the Joe Toth case. I was the lead investigator."

"Do it anyway," Jenny commanded.

Lem looked at Jenny with condescension, but walked to a desk and punched in a few commands. "Well, I'm sure there's nothing here I don't know about, but I'll read through it when I'm entering in this new information."

"We'll wait."

"No we won't," Grace said. "Let's be on our way. We've got a long trip ahead."

"Where to? Are you heading back to Berkeley? Better leave me your contact information. What if I find out something? Don't you want me to get back in touch?"

"Yes, please do that." Grace handed her card to Lem. "Be sure to enter this into the electronic file."

"Yes, ma'am."

"Thank you, Lem."

"Yes ma'am. That's what we're here for."

As Jenny and Grace exited the police station, Jenny dropped a dab-move, which Lem noticed, but was not sure what he had just seen. After they were underway, Jenny said, "That guy was only interested in the past, not the future."

"How do you mean?"

"Well, he's proud of their effort to find Giuseppe. He's proud of their filing system. He's proud of himself. But he has nothing to say about how they might pursue this new information."

"He did suggest the possibility that father and son might be reunited in some exotic place."

"That's a pile of crap, and he knew it when he said it."

Grace could feel her face flush. She had thought the suggestion had some merit. "Why in the world would you say that?"

"Everything we've heard goes against that possibility. They weren't close. It seems pretty evident to me that, like his mother, Roscoe is a gold digger and loves the situation he's now entrenched in. That guy Lem watches too many movies."

"Okay. I think you're probably right, but that's no reason to entirely reject the possibility."

"I'll keep it in the part of my brain where I store low-likelihood things."

ॐ

Roscoe's cabin was eight miles northeast of the Jepson ranch house. It did not belong to him, but at one time it was probably a miners shelter. It had, over the years been taken over by mammals, reptiles, insects, and Roscoe. It took him about twenty minutes to get there on a 50cc Honda dirt bike that he kept hidden on BLM land near an undeveloped corner of the Jepson property. He had a camp stove, a cot, and a down bag. Each time he left the ranch house, he took a supply of groceries with him. He heated up a can of Dinty Moore beef stew, and when he was finished, found a sliver of sunlight where he sat down and lit up a Macanudo Maduro. In his lap was a large tray on which were the drawings of his grand scheme.

ॐ

On Sunday morning Amy Toth, wearing a light blue terrycloth bathrobe, heard a knock on her door. When she peeked through the peephole she saw a uniformed policeman that she had gone to high school with. She tightened the bathrobe sash and opened the door a crack. "Hi, Kenny."

"Morning, Ms. Toth. May I come in? I've got a few questions I'd like to ask you."

"Well, if you must. What's going on?"

"Were you at the Cornfield Cages on Friday?"

"No. What are they?"

"It's a batting range on the east side."

"I don't know what a batting range is. Friday night I was still in Omaha."

"Anyone see you over there?"

Amy considered the question, and finally said, "Of course not Kenny, how could anybody see me? I always become invisible when I get into Nebraska. What's this about? It's eight o'clock in the morning."

"What do you mean about becoming invisible?"

"What do you mean when you asked if anybody saw me? How can anybody be anyplace without being seen?"

"If you were in Omaha, we'd like to be able to verify that."

"Kenny, what in the hell are you talking about? I'm about to ask you to leave."

"Yesterday morning a guy was found over at the batting range. Someone apparently whacked him with a bat sometime Friday night and killed him."

"I still don't know what a batting range is. And I sure as hell don't know why you would want to talk to me about it."

"Your name was on the client register."

"Well, Kenny, I don't know how it got there, I don't know what a batting range is, and I was in Omaha."

"Why were you in Omaha?"

"Because my daughter and her husband live there and they invited me to come over and spend a week with them during semester break."

"Can they verify that?"

"Are you kidding me? I used to think you got good grades in school. What is it with you?"

Kenny handed her a pad. "You're going to have to give me their names."

"Find them yourself, Kenny. I don't even know what you're talking about, and I still don't know what a batting range is."

CHAPTER TWENTY

It was 9:35 when the women awoke the next morning. The trip south had been relatively quick, given the season and the late hour of departure. By the time they'd had found a few edible morsels and were in their beds, it was past midnight.

"What today?" asked Jenny.

"I want to check in with the cops in Richmond where I filed my report about Roscoe. Then I need to get over to my office and get a couple things done. I can show you some of the stuff I've been telling you about. I think Rocky was right that I need to look for another assistant."

At the Richmond Police station, Grace asked if there had been any progress in the missing person investigation involving Roscoe Toth. A clerk disappeared for what seemed like fifteen or twenty minutes and finally returned to tell Grace there was nothing new. No leads.

Grace gave the guy an exasperated look, but said nothing.

"Sorry ma'am," the guy said after a long pause.

"Are you doing anything?"

"I have to tell you, ma'am. Right now we have some activities that are higher priority than this. But we have the file, and the guy who is assigned will work it as time permits."

"He has family in Dufur, Oregon. Here's a phone number where they can be reached. It seems to me that the first step should be to call them and find out if they know anything."

"Thanks, ma'am. I'll leave it with Elija. He's assigned to your case."

117

"Do you still have my number?"

"Yes, ma'am."

"Okay." Then, softly aside to Jenny, "Let's get out of here."

Grace's office was in an industrial area not far from the Chevron refinery offices. Her desk was in the corner of an open room with lab tables and equipment filling the balance of the space. A water system was carried by overhead piping and there were also natural gas pipelines leading to various outlets around the perimeter.

Jenny immediately spied an array of screened cages swarming with insects of all descriptions. After watching them for several minutes, she said, "So these are the creatures that you know how to attract and kill?"

"That they are, and I need to feed them." One by one, Grace opened access ports on each cage and dropped in very unappetizing potions. *One man's poison*, Jenny thought, as the insects swarmed to the new goodies.

"Every one of these insects is a pest. If there were no human beings on earth, which was the case when they evolved, they would not be pests, but each one is destructive to human life in some way. The global population of most of these cute little creatures is more than twice what it was before the evolution of human life as we know it. This little guy thrives in wheat fields, for example. These mosquitoes hatch in the rooting holes left by wild pigs in Hawaii – a human introduction. They are spreading avian malaria which is causing serious depletion to the native bird populations there. These little fellows are what we call bedbugs. Not something you want to find in their favorite hiding place."

Grace went to a refrigerated cabinet and retrieved a vial containing not more than a cc of dark liquid. When she uncorked it all the bedbugs quit their feeding and hurried to the side of the cage where Grace was holding the vial. Grace then backed away until she was some 50 feet from the cage. The bugs stayed in place. After she capped the vial and returned it to the refrigeration unit, the bugs slowly returned to their feeding activity.

"Awesome," Jenny said, almost gasping as she said it. "If you had told me that would happen, I wouldn't have believed it, or even if I believed that some would react, I never would have guessed that the whole cage full would do that. I still can't believe you mixed up a batch of something that would cause that to happen."

"That's why the death threat story is at least somewhat be-lievable."

Jenny went to a cage filled with grasshoppers. What's so bad about these? They're kind of pretty."

"Again, they've been around for eons, but because they thrive on cultivated crops, their populations since the advent of agriculture is much bigger than it was historically. Para-doxically, humans create the habitat by growing crops. The pest populations grow, and finally the beasts get so plentiful that they destroy the very crop that caused their population to explode."

"That's a pretty interesting concept, Gracie."

"The reality is, most animal populations have cyclical abundance patterns. Among food, water, predation, shelter, disease, climate or any one of various other needs, often spe-cific to the organism, there is always one single limiting fac-tor – one specific deficit that determines how many individu-als that particular ecosystem will support. Variations in that one factor are what cause the abundance cycles."

"This guy Jeff, who dropped me off at the casino where I met you, was talking to me about rabbits and foxes being on a 'teeterboard,' as he called it. He was an interesting guy. Smart, but never schooled."

"Well the tendency to keep habitat in a state of semi-de-struction is very common among animal populations – hu-man beings included. The difference with humans is that we keep finding temporary patches – ways to remedy an immediate deficiency. The populations keep growing and eventually there will be such over-use of resources that the only answer will be for dominant civilizations to eliminate some other human culture to get their resources. The little pipsqueak in North Korea seems to be on the verge of something like that right now."

"How about all these black widows?"

"I can't really say that human activity has been a benefit to black widow populations. But my thinking is who would give a shit if every black widow on earth were to disappear. I'm pretty sure that widows are not responsible for controlling any other population in a predatory sense. They're just a nuisance. Rats, the same. I haven't started any rat pheromone studies. That would probably be something that mimicked a glandular secretion produced as a sexual attractant. Given enough time and a threat-free chance to keep up the work I'm doing here, we can rid the world of vermin."

"Grace, this stuff you're doing was interesting when you told me about it, but seeing your lab, and seeing how this stuff actually works is awesome. You'll be a national hero – maybe even a global one. Nobody will ever believe that I know the person who is destined to become the *Time* magazine person of the year. I should get your autograph right now. I should get a bunch in fact so I can sell them on ebay."

"I must agree. It is a very promising situation. You've helped me a lot over the last few days. When we met, I was so shaken up about Roscoe's death threat that I was actually thinking about shutting down the whole operation. Seriously, I was scared half to death, as I'm sure you could tell."

"We still haven't found much out, but it does appear that we can relax a little."

Grace had a land line phone on her office desk. At that moment, it rang.

"Here comes your death threat," Jenny said, regretting it even as she said it. *What if it is,* she thought. *I'd never recover.*

Grace picked up the phone, and after two *yeses,* two loud *I don't knows* and an *okay* spaced at varying intervals, she replaced the receiver.

"Tell me it wasn't. Please."

"Don't worry. It wasn't. It was my ex wanting to know why my lender had called him. I really don't know what's going on."

"Had you thought of what to say in case it was a threat?"

"I *have* given it some thought, but no, I wouldn't have been ready for that."

"Tell me this, Grace. What would you have done if it had been Roscoe telling you he was all right and wanted to come back to work?"

"I would have asked him a lot of questions to find out what he has been up to, but if he wanted to come back, I would have said *no.*"

"Even if he begged?"

"Even if he begged."

"Good for you, Grace. Show him who's boss."

Grace stoked her chin as if she had a beard. "What are you going to major in?"

"You'll probably laugh, but I'm thinking criminology."

"I doubt you'll graduate in time to solve our case, Jenny."

"I know. I just see a niche. I'm not sure. It just seems like I've been having a brush with crime situations recently, and I find it fascinating."

"Go for it. You have the analytical mind for it. Your approach would also work in my little world here. How are you going to pay for school?"

"I don't know. My mom is going to help. I figure on getting loans."

"How about coming to work here?"

"Right here? You mean work for you?"

"Yep. For me."

"That would be more awesome than I could even have imagined, Grace. Thank you."

CHAPTER TWENTY-ONE

Knowing that Larry Jepson's schedule, which seldom varied, would not permit a visit to the ranch house that day, Roscoe mentally mapped today's agenda. When Larry Jepson had first agreed to fund Ross Jepson's wild rice plan, Larry had told Ross that he did not want him to manage the construction in person. He knew that Ross was so meticulous and demanding that the project would take forever if Ross was around to manage it. They agreed to a schedule wherein Ross would send updated drawings to Larry. Ross was so opposed to the idea of leaving oversight to Larry that they finally struck a compromise in which Larry would allow him to visit one week-end day each month to view progress and inspect the work. That had proven successful during the past six-month period when the initial construction was underway. But as the project neared completion, Roscoe needed to be able to tweak the plans without having to explain the reasons to Larry.

To enable his being on the project site on a more regular basis, Roscoe needed to quit his job with Grace Summers's pesticide investigations without explaining to her what his reasons were. He did not want her to interrogate him about his foray into the wild rice business, and he didn't want her to know where he was going to be doing it. He knew that early in his employ with her, he had mentioned having lived on a wheat farm in Dufur, but he thought that Grace would probably not remember that detail. Ordinarily, a precise planner, on this occasion, almost on an impulse, Roscoe thought up the death threat story and then disappeared. He failed to grasp the effect that this story would have on Grace. Certainly, it never crossed his mind that she would be frightened and conclude that she might be next. Roscoe just wanted to disappear without any discussion. He found the death threat story very amusing and knew that Grace would believe it because she was so impressed by her own success in her business.

All of this enabled him to move surreptitiously into his old deteriorating cabin on a hillside densely covered with juniper and tall sage brush. The BLM parcel overlooked the Deschutes River, the river that would make his "wild rice" project become a reality. His mother knew he was hiding out there and agreed with Ross's assessment that it was a good way to personally manage the project. In addition to Larry's repetitive agenda, Ross's mother would call him when there was some change – one which would cause Larry to be on site when he normally would be gone, or the reverse, which would open the door for Roscoe visit the construction crew.

Today he had work to do at his lair. Tomorrow he would have a free run of the project area where his wild rice facilities were taking shape. His drawings had been developed to the extent that the construction was advancing nicely, but many details were still needed to keep the contractors busy. The weather was dry, around thirty-five degrees. Roscoe put on a jacket and arranged his beach chair in a flat spot where the sun would hit him. With his drawing board in his lap, he began making detail panels for his effluent canal, and completed some of the interior components that would be on next week's construction agenda. His drawings, done without a straight edge or scaling ruler of any kind were perfect, as were his printed notes. His first design had not included a settling pond. He since had realized that one was essential to his needs. Roscoe had traced the contours of the project site from a USGS topo map. Using the contours as guides he drew out a plan for a lake that would cover about two acres. The dam in the gulch leading down to the Deschutes River would be six feet at the high point and around thirty feet across. From there the sediment-free water would flow out through a wooden flume with weirs at intervals varying from twenty-five to fifty feet depending on the grade. He drew top, front, and side views for the weir detail, and on his overview of the project site, he showed the half-mile pathway that the flume would follow down to the river.

He already had given conceptual drawings to the EPA and to the Oregon fisheries agency. Some of the details he was now working on would make the facilities different, but once they were approved no one would ever know if they were built exactly as designed. So Roscoe felt no need to re-submit any of the plans. He knew in fact that if he showed his current design to either agency they would not permit it.

His vantage point at the cabin gave him a view not only of the great river, but of the portion of the ranch where the construction was under way. The scene gave him a sense of command and superiority.

CHAPTER TWENTY-TWO

Giuseppe and Margo Toth moved to New York from Hungary when Roscoe was a four-year-old. Joe, as he wished to be called as soon as he set foot on the jetway at JFK International, had been peripherally involved in lending and numbers operations with the Slovak mafia. In spite of being a man of small stature he had ways of being persuasive. It was not unusual for him to carry a small .32 caliber Beretta, for example. He was hired to visit delinquent debtors and had an excellent record of success, which caused him to be respected by the operators that hired him. He made good money until the operators disappeared. The word that came down to Giuseppe was that the Russian mafia had taken over the landscape that theretofore had been the sole proprietorship of the Slovaks. Giuseppe visited the US Embassy in Budapest and got the necessary clearances under the Refugee Act of 1980 to flee with his wife to the US.

Joe fully intended to exit his life of crime. Upon arriving in New York he attended the ABC Bartending School, graduating with honors. The graduation ceremony was not a solemn affair, and Joe knew immediately that he'd found a profession that he would enjoy. After he'd worked the Alley Cat Lounge for a year, he asked for the two week vacation he'd earned and took a quick, well designed journey that he hoped would satisfy his curiosity to see what life was like in the western United States. His primary co-worker at the Alley Cat was an aspiring thespian who had migrated east from

Portland, Oregon. A self-professed expert sailboard enthusiast, he resolutely insisted that Joe spend a night in the town of Hood River on the Columbia.

Although Joe never took up the sport of sailboarding, he saw in it a lifestyle that was carefree and exciting. Leaving Margo and Roscoe in their hotel room, he closed the bar at the City Saloon, where he told stories of his boyhood and young adult life that not only captivated the bartender but held the patrons in rapt disbelief. Before the evening was over the guy behind the bar, Wes Demeter, had called the tavern in Dufur which he thought had an opening. He was right. Wes told Cindy Wilson, the owner and very often the tender there, that he had the perfect man for the job. Joe Toth never returned to New York.

Joe loved his work at the tavern and most of the patrons who frequented the place. Many were members of a local biker group, "The Free Souls." After he'd tended the bar for a year, he was invited to join the club, at which time he bought himself a Harley Softail Fat Boy. From that day on he became a somewhat rare visitor to his own home.

As it became known around Dufur, The Dalles, and even Hood River that it was worth the price of a few beers just to listen to the new tender's stories, the clientele grew. Some of the stories may have been made up, but all were entertaining. Joe had other talents, as well. He could make music with anything that he could pick up, and when he was not serving, he was performing. Cindy Wilson could see that her business was thriving, but she also noted that her wine orders came in short. Either that, or some of the cases were disappearing. She spoke to Joe about it, and he told her that he would keep a careful watch on the storage room.

Cindy's boyfriend was himself a Soul member named Chance Chambers. Chance enjoyed Joe's jester-like antics, and the two of them became buddies, but at the same time

Chance had to walk the fine line between their friendship and Cindy's suspicions of Joe.

Margo and Roscoe lived in a doublewide on Fifteenmile Creek east of Dufur. Joe bought the lot as soon as he had enough money, which was six months after their arrival. Joe loved the commute to and from work on his Harley and had no trouble covering the twelve miles in ten minutes. He also enjoyed the camaraderie of the club members and often joined them for after-hours parties and journeys. He grew his black hair to shoulder-length and a beard that to his delight grew in gray. Joe's charm was appreciated by the clubbers and he cherished the recognition.

Cindy grew more and more certain that Joe was responsible for the disappearance of her wine. Finally, Chance confronted Joe at the after-hours club. Chance told Joe that if he ever found out that Joe had taken even one bottle of wine from the inventory, Joe would feel it. Joe smiled, denied that he had ever taken any wine from the bar, and gave Chance a bottle of Chateau Latour. "I have no use for the plebeian wines that Cindy serves in the bar." Chance didn't know whether Joe was being straight with him or not, but he could not stay mad at this guy.

At the conclusion of his shift behind the bar, Joe would either ride his Harley back to the trailer on Fifteenmile Creek, or he would entertain girls at a clubhouse the Souls kept in The Dalles. Sometimes he would spend the night there, and sometimes he would ride home, arriving in the morning about the time Margo was getting ready to take Roscoe to school.

Meanwhile, Roscoe grew more and more frightened of his new environment. On one occasion, he saw a bear at the river with two cubs. After that, he would not leave the trailer except to go to school.

Going off to school was exciting to Roscoe. He was a year older than his classmates, a result of his parents migration from Hungary through New York to Dufur, Oregon. He made a few friends, but perhaps more importantly, he had a teacher who recognized his advanced intelligence and challenged him with special projects that Roscoe found fascinating. He did very well in school and became an avid reader. Each day after school his mother would pick him up and drive him back to their doublewide where he would work on his extra assignments or learn the things that his mother occupied herself with – knitting, watercolor painting, and crossword puzzles, for example. Often the two of them engaged in these activities together; so it seemed a natural extension of their close alliance when Roscoe would seek the safety of crawling into his mother's bed.

That had started after the bear incident, and it seemed natural enough to Margo that it became fairly common. If Joe came home, Roscoe would go to his own bed without complaining, but would feel frightened and would imagine scenes in which the bear would eat his father.

Margo, a lithe, dark-eyed seductress, was comforted by little Roscoe's presence, but she found a couple of men in town who appreciated her eagerness to let them please her. So, after dropping Roscoe at school, she often would have a liaison, sometimes two, with local citizens. One such lucky man, if only rarely, was Lawrence Jepson.

Margo was discrete, and although she was occasionally the subject of rumors, she was known to be unfaithful only by the scant few with whom she would liaise. Roscoe, himself, never heard the rumors.

One evening over dinner, when Roscoe was twelve years old, Margo said, "Roscoe, there's something I need to tell you."

"Well, I'm sitting right across the table from you, why don't you go ahead and tell me then?"

"I have been seeing Mr Jepson."

"Do you like him better than you like me?"

"No, but he's richer," Margo said with a smile.

"Does he buy you things?"

"No. Not now, but imagine how rich we'd be if I had married Mr. Jepson instead of your dad."

"Imagine how rich we'd be if I played basketball in the NBA. Same deal. No chance of either one happening."

"You are absolutely right. No chance. Not unless your dad were to die, I guess. And that's not likely to happen."

"Well, let's put it this way. Everybody dies. It's just that usually you can tell when it's about to happen, because they become old and frail. Dad is young and hearty."

"Yes, he is. I guess I'm just thinking about something that will never come true."

After that conversation, Roscoe's dream of the bear eating his father began to recur on a fairly regular basis. Sometimes Joe seemed to slide down the bear's throat effortlessly, and other times a bloody battle between Joe and the bear would seem to last forever. At first Roscoe thought of the dreams as nightmares, but over time he began to look forward to them to see what form the kill and consumption might take. He particularly enjoyed one in which the bear leisurely ate the limbs one by one, appearing to smile at the sun as he would swallow each appendage.

But all the dreams stopped when Roscoe was thirteen years old and Joe Toth disappeared. Five and a half years later, when Roscoe turned eighteen, Margo married Larry Jepson in a private ceremony on the left bank of the Deschutes River. That same spot would later be the outfall site of Roscoe's wild rice effluent. Under the Oregon *Death in Absentia* law, Giuseppe Toth had been declared dead.

CHAPTER TWENTY-THREE

After Grace had offered Jenny a job, she commenced in earnest to show Jenny each of the sophisticated analytic devices that Jenny would have to learn how to operate. In a general overview she explained sequences of discovery in the development process and moved on to an explanation of what she saw as a production schedule. A few glitches needed to be corrected before they could go into business. In fact the prototype for most of the products were combined in a way that could not be sustained in mass production. So Jenny would be involved both in analytic work and eventually in helping to devise methodologies for full scale production of the pheromone pest control creations.

"There's something I'd like to discuss with you, Jenny," Grace said after several hours of talking about the business and the tasks at hand.

Jenny smiled and nodded.

"What would you think of starting your university career next September instead of the spring semester. I really need a lot of help. You'll be able to save some money – especially since you'd be living with me – and we could continue to follow this mystery that we seem to be involved with."

"Living with you?"

"That would be a fringe benefit of the job here."

"Holy guacamole. You really are a convincing recruiter."

"What do you think?"

"You must know I'm not just going to say it's fine with me. I've got to give this whole thing some thought."

"I know, and I think that's the appropriate approach. Let's go back to my place and have some dinner."

"One point comes to mind that bears on my decision. What would your rules be with respect to any dates I might have or any boyfriends that might chance to become part of my life?"

"Treat my house with respect, be responsible to yourself, and pay me the courtesy of giving me some advance warning about things that I should be warned about. Would that be too strict?"

"No. That works. Thanks, Grace. My gosh, that is so very generous of you. I don't know when I've ever felt so valued by anyone."

"What about waiting until fall semester to enroll?"

"I wouldn't mind doing that. I'd want to check with the big U to see if they allow me to postpone my admission and get out of my dorm reservation."

"I can probably help, if you need it. It sounds like in principle you're in agreement."

"Yeah, I'd say so. I'm thinkin' that if I could solve a crime, and then get into a criminology major, I would be sort of like a seasoned student – sort of like a star of the program, don't you think? I mean all the other crim students would be whispering, 'Hey, that's Jennifer Lindsey. She solved a real crime.' I'm thinking I might get a tattoo on my arm that says, *I solved one.*"

"I'm happy to hear you've thought this whole situation through so thoroughly. Sounds like you'll be a natural for detective work. And that being the case, where do we go from here?"

"Grace, as my mother used to say, 'I just don't know.' I'll say this, though. I'm still on III. B. of my outline. That's the assumption that Roscoe did not get a call, made up the story, and has gone into hiding somewhere. I will also say I don't think he's sojourning on a tropical isle with Giuseppe. Roscoe is somewhere doing something that he planned long ago. How do I know? I don't. It's just what we thought before, and I still do."

"Okay, so do I. Where do we go next?"

"Well, a couple of options: 1) Call Lou Ferry and ask if he's heard anything; 2) Call Ms. Jepson and see if she gives us the same story as Mr. Jepson; 3) Wait for someone to call you. That could be Ferry or either of the two police stations we visited."

"Let's go back home. I'm tired and hungry."

Grace's desk phone rang.

"Hey, maybe that's Roscoe calling to apologize and tell you where he is."

"Not likely," Grace mumbled as she picked up the phone. "Hello?"

"Ms. Summers, this is Lem Russell."

Grace tried to hide her excitement. "Oh, hi, Lem. How are things in the Columbia Gorge today?

"Fine, Ms. Summers. Cloudy and a cooler, as the weather bird says."

"What occasions your call, Lem?"

"Well, I don't think this is significant, but I did promise to let you know if I heard anything."

"Well, thanks, Lem. We were just wondering about this mystery."

"I had to sign a document today that had Mr. Jepson's name on it."

"What was the document?"

"ODFW – that's fish and game up here, ODEQ, and the Portland District Corps of Engineers wanted my okay on an outfall for a wild rice farm owned by Jepson. I went ahead and signed the sumbitch. They'd all signed off on it, so I didn't see why I shouldn't."

"Which agency originated the permit you okayed?"

"I think it starts with the Corps of Engineers."

"Can you give me a number for them? I might want to talk to somebody over there."

"Sure, Ms. Summers, Lem said. He gave her a number and said, "Talk to Bruce Bennett over there in their EQ Branch."

"Thanks for your heads-up, Lem, I'm glad you're keeping us in mind."

"Okay, Ma'am. How's yer cute little friend doin'?"

"Okay, Lem. I'll let her know you asked after her."

She hung up and said to Jenny, "Lem Russell wants to know how you're doin'."

"I'll call him back and tell him I'm doin' pretty good. So what's new with Lem?"

"A permit for Larry Jepson's rice water effluent came across his desk. He told me he signed it because everybody else had. Do you know what lemmings are? Well, Lem has a little lemming in him."

"At least he called you, that's a great sign."

"True. I think I'll call this guy at the Corps and see what he might know."

ॐ

When Grace dialed the 503 number, a melodic voice on the other end sang "Bruce Bennett."

"Mr. Bennett, my name is Grace Summers. I'm calling about a permit that the Corps of Engineers is issuing for a wild rice effluent of some kind near The Dalles."

"I'd have to look that up," Bennett replied now all business.

Grace waited for over a minute before saying, "Making any progress?"

"On what?"

"Looking up the permit."

"I'm sorry, I didn't know you wanted me to look it up."

Grace Summers's first inclination was to ask Bruce if it was dark where his head currently resided. Instead, she hung up. Grace was aware of the Army Corps of Engineers permit procedures from having needed a permit for one of her own projects. She knew that the Corps must handle hundreds of them every day and felt a certain amount of sympathy for anyone who had to deal with this red tape operation; but she was incensed at Bennett's apparent unawareness of how he should have handled her phone call. After a five minute cool-down period, she called back and in the same intonation heard, "Bruce Bennett."

"Will you kindly send me a copy of any permit that you have sent out for review for the wild rice farming effluent near The Dalles?"

"Is this Ms. Summers?"

"Yes."

"I'm sorry, I guess we got cut off. I will certainly make sure that gets sent out to you, Ms. Summers."

"Do it yourself, Bruce. Don't just see that it gets done. Time may be of the essence. Just do it."

"Surely, may I get your address?"

"For Christ's sake Bruce, of course you can. How would you send it out otherwise?" Grace gave Bruce the address of her laboratory, and hung up. With an aggravated exhale, she said to Jenny, "It's good for this great country of ours that Bruce Bennett's service in the United States Army is in a civilian capacity."

Jenny laughed. Let's go to the grocery store. I'll buy the stuff and cook our dinner tonight."

CHAPTER TWENTY-FOUR

As a part of gearing Jenny up for her new job as Lab Tech in her pheromone factory, Grace got Jenny an iPhone and put her on the lab cellular account. Jenny's first call was to Kathy in Ames. "Hey, I got a job."

"Where?"

"Working at Grace's pesticide lab. She's been so kind. I just *can not* believe the incredible good fortune that has befallen me on me trip. Oh, and by the way, I'm not going to start school at Cal until next September, so if you and your dad come out next summer we'll have no distraction. We can go up to Tahoe or something."

"Excellent. I'll have to keep working on Dad."

After ten minutes or so, they concluded the call, and Jenny asked Grace if she'd heard her comment about the good fortune. "That's mainly you, Grace," Jenny said. "I'm forever beholden."

ဆ

Of all the courses that Roscoe took in his organic chemistry major, his favorite was an elective – ichthyology. The first thing that attracted him to the course was the instructor, Dr. Melissa Perry, who Roscoe called Missy in spite of her scolding requests for him to stop. He also liked the course itself, and in particular the life history of the five species of Pacific salmon that spawn in North America. When the semester ended, he bought four bottles of Gucci *Guilty Absolute Eau de Parfum* and gave one of them to Missy. Missy, eight years older than Roscoe, thanked him and told him he could now call her Missy if he wished. This thrilled Roscoe, who imagined a frisky liaison with Missy. They never saw each other again.

The following summer – already four years ago – he had told his parents that he might want to somehow make a career out of salmon fishing, or perhaps salmon rearing. He took a break from his duties on the wheat farm and visited two hatcheries on the Columbia River – the big facility at Bonneville plus the Oxbow Salmon Hatchery at Cascade Locks. By exhaustive interrogation of the personnel at the hatcheries Roscoe obtained a first hand knowledge of what he would need to know if he decided to pursue his interest in the salmon business. Upon returning from the overnight trip he gave his mother a bottle of Gucci *Guilty Absolute Eau de Parfum*. Margo was delighted. He kept two for a future project.

"Mother," Roscoe told her, "You have married into a life of opulence. Think of how it used to be in that trailer. We were groveling. Now we are among the most respected people in Dufur, Oregon. Dufur, Oregon. Think of that. The world is our oyster. Anything we want is ours."

∞

On Thursdays, Larry Jepson always traveled to Portland. The local wheat farmers had set up Thursdays as the day they scheduled council meetings, auctions, Rotary gatherings and so on. Most of them used the time in Portland to stock up on any needs that they might have on their respective ranches. As a result, Larry was away from his wheat farm from about seven or so in the morning to around five in the evening.

The construction of Roscoe's wild rice project facilities had reached a point where Roscoe needed to discuss design changes with the contractors. Roscoe hated it when Larry looked over his shoulder and asked questions. More important, at least for now, he did not want Larry to know he was around. So when he saw Larry drive out, Roscoe gathered up his new drawings and spec sheets, hopped onto his Honda, and rode down to the ranch house.

After greeting his mother, Roscoe walked down the hill to where the construction crew was beginning to assemble. It was not a day too soon, for the work plan for the day included pouring concrete in some places that Roscoe wanted changed to wood. "Can you cancel the redi-mix delivery?" Roscoe asked the foreman.

"Not likely."

"Well, try. The permit review agencies want us to change the effluent canal to a covered flume," he lied. "Get on the phone and cancel the truck."

"Roscoe, the forms and rebar are in place. We're pouring today."

"Tell it to the Corps of Engineers. That's who wants wood."

"I don't believe those assholes."

"True, but you never know who requires the changes, there's so many reviewers."

"They're all *assholes*," the foreman said earnestly. He looked toward the crew beginning to assemble the final rebar placements in the effluent structure. "Stop with the rebar," he yelled. "We got a change order."

Roscoe laid his new drawings on a sawhorse and explained to the foreman that the effluent structure would now be constructed of pressure treated lumber and would be covered. He asked the guy if he could interpret the drawings.

"Why the weirs?"

"Okay, we've got this two acre pond as a settling basin," Roscoe explained, waving his hand in a sweeping gesture. "The permit reviewers did not think that was sufficient to keep sediments out of the river so they're asking for weirs. Each step in the ladder-like array will allow more of the sediments to drop out of the water before it is finally discharged into the river. It's a pain because we'll have to clean out the flume every year."

"Okay, Roscoe, if that's what you want. I think there were six trucks in your redi-mix order. I hope for your sake they'll be willing to cancel."

"When you tell 'em it's for the Jepson contract they will do it. If they say no, let me talk to them."

When Roscoe returned to the ranch house he asked his mother, "Do you have any idea how Larry ever managed to get this huge piece of property?"

"I'm pretty sure it's been in his family for years – generations. Why."

"I was just thinking how cool it would be to own something like this. I mean, we live here, but we don't own it."

"Well, I assume I own half of it. After all, I'm married to Larry. I think the ranch becomes community property."

"You're probably right. I just think it would be better to own the whole thing."

"We're where we want to be, Ross. Don't get any bright ideas."

જી

Roscoe already had one.

CHAPTER TWENTY-FIVE

When the mail arrived at Grace's lab three days later, there was an envelope from the Portland District of the Corps of Engineers. Inside were two permit applications: one for an effluent structure into the Deschutes River and the other for discharge from the structure. "Look what I got."

Jenny quickly walked to Grace's desk and looked at the papers that Grace handed her.

"Kind of difficult to interpret."

"True. Jenny, would you read this stuff as though you were going to be tested on it and see if anything tweaks your curiosity?"

"Sure. I'll make marks where I don't understand something. By the way, do you have a name for your company?"

"So far, on all my paper work I've just been calling it Summers Pest Control."

"How about The Graceful Death."

Grace tilted her head slightly as she considered the name. Finally she said, "Very nice. I like that." Grace really did. She wrote the suggested name in a spiral notebook on her desk.

Jenny pored over both permits, knowing that there were aspects that she did not understand. She now occupied Roscoe's former desk. Grace had deleted some material from a Lenovo laptop that Roscoe had used and had installed some hardware that Jenny would need when she was up to speed on her tasks. After about an hour Jenny said to Grace, "I think it's going to be key to look up whatever I can about wild rice production."

"Feel free. Whatever it takes to get an idea about what's going on at Jepson's place. What I'm hoping to interpret from these is whether they're legit or not. If they're not, then we might begin to wonder if Roscoe could be up to something. We have to be careful about concluding things about Roscoe. We don't even know if he's alive or not."

"Okay, I'll look for inconsistencies."

Jenny googled wild rice production and sat at her desk for another hour reading articles and making notes on a yellow note pad. All she knew about wild rice growing in the US until now was what Larry Jepson had told them when they visited his wheat farm. By the time Jenny had read enough to have a fuller understanding of the industry she felt fairly certain that Jepson was either lying, or that he was simply repeating something that he had been told. Finally, she called to Grace, "I can talk to you about the permits, whenever you're ready."

"Now is fine."

Without getting out of her chair, Jenny rolled it across the room to Grace's desk. Holding up the two permits, she said, "Well, these things are either incomplete or not consistent with what I now know about wild rice production."

"Let's go over what you found out."

"Okay. Jepson told us that the seed needs to be frozen before it is sown. That part is true. What he did not mention is how it is grown. It's grown in flooded fields, just like Chinese rice – the white kind. Almost all the cultivated wild rice is grown in California. I couldn't find any record of harvest in Oregon.

"Jepson's permit applications show a two acre pond just outside of the building, that's designated as a settling basin. The effluent canal emerges from the settling pond and runs to the Deschutes about a mile upstream from the Columbia. The

141

implication of the permit is that whatever is happening inside the building is going to create this silt-containing runoff. I just couldn't find anything in my reading about wild rice that would involve a building and the substantial runoff that the permit specifies. That building was huge. I can't believe that you need a building like that to freeze wild rice seed.

"Beyond that, Jepson's wheat fields are growing on gently rolling land that even without any experience I can tell is not suited to flooding. The way I see it, those overhead sprinkling contraptions are the only way he can irrigate. He would have to build levees all around his property in order to flood them. I'm thinking it would be impossible. You're intuition to look over these permits was right on target, Grace."

"I just had a hunch that it would turn out that way, but I still don't know what we do we do about it? We don't know much about Jepson. Maybe he's the one with something up his sleeve."

"I really doubt that. Jepson wasn't all that forthcoming with information, but when we finally got him talking he didn't act like he was hiding anything."

"Well, Jenny, the thing is, if he was, he wouldn't act like he was. If you're a person who does sneaky things, you get good at looking honest. In fact it may be that his evasive manner when we first got there is the most convincing argument that he wasn't lying."

"So what do we do now?"

"That's the big question. I think we have to proceed with our work here at The Graceful Death. I can't just forego my whole program to find out what happened to Roscoe."

"Wait. At this point it goes beyond just finding out what happened to him. It looks like the guy is up to some kind of skulduggery. We've got to find out what it is."

"No we don't. I've got to figure out how to mass produce my pheromone pest elimination systems before I run out of money."

ℬ

The procedures used to analyze the atomic composition of compounds they were working with, and the machinery that Grace had to accomplish those analyses were fascinating to Jenny. She considered the process analogous to her new fascination with solving mysteries. She was quick to learn how to operate the sophisticated equipment, and each day she became better able to anticipate the work plan and to function not only independently, but effectively. On several occasions Grace remarked on the fortunate coincidence of their meeting and the unlikeliness of Grace acquiescing to offer Jenny a ride. "The unexpected turns in the evolution of events is one of the things that makes life precious," she said.

Jenny's pay was not equivalent to her contribution and Grace let her know that if she could stick with the job through the coming months Grace would be able to give her a raise.

"Give me a break," Jenny exclaimed on one such occasion. "You're giving me free room and board. That's got to be worth a couple thou a month, and I'm probably underestimating."

"I just want you to know that your job performance has been excellent, and you are appreciated."

By using computer search engines Jenny was able to educate herself on some of the difficulties that Grace faced before she could go into production. While she did not have the educational background to offer technical suggestions, she did on occasion see situations that could be altered slightly to enable quicker results for a given task.

In the course of using her Lenovo laptop she discovered a number of personal files that clearly were left there by Roscoe. Among his bookmarked pages were a number of bulletin boards discussing such things as automotive repair, fishing, carpentry, beer making, and a few other subjects. Also bookmarked were websites for purchasing various items. There were several for cigars. Perhaps most interesting to Jenny were two dating or introduction websites. During her lunch break she would occasionally try to get a better profile of Roscoe by looking at his browsing history.

One evening as they were eating a Chinese chicken salad at Grace's home, Jenny asked, "Did Roscoe smoke cigars?"

"I never saw him smoking, but I only saw him when he was at work," Grace replied.

"How about dating? Did he ever talk about his social life to you?"

"Nope, he was pretty private."

"Did he ever hit on you?"

"You mean did he come on to me as if to get some level of personal involvement?"

"Um… yeah, that's what I mean, Grace."

"Nope. If he did, I wasn't aware of it. Why are you asking?"

"I've been looking at his computer files. He didn't protect any of his private stuff with passwords, so his browse history is easy to check out. Anyway, he was a member of a couple of dating websites. Two to be exact."

"A couple always means two."

"I know, I just wanted to let you know that I was using the word correctly. Anyway, I have been trying to put together a sort of profile of what Roscoe is like. Remember, you knew the guy, but I didn't."

"Oh yeah, I do remember that, now that you mention it." Grace took a sip of the chilled Chardonnay she was drinking with her dinner.

"Okay. Okay. If you'll quit making fun of me, you might find some interest in what I'm saying."

Grace did derive some pleasure in toying with her teenage friend, so, knowing that Jenny was almost effervescing with an urge to tell her something, she continued to eat without responding.

"Ha ha," Jenny enunciated. "So if you don't want to know, I won't tell you."

Grace knew she would, so kept on eating. "How do you like the salad?"

"All right, Father, knock it off," Jenny blurted.

"I'm dying to find out what you know, Jenny. Just having some fun."

"How old is Roscoe, anyway? He presents himself as twenty-six."

"I expect that's about right."

"In his preferences – that's where you identify what traits you want in your date or new acquaintance – he has forty to fifty for the age. I mean, wow. His own mother must be around that age. I don't get it."

"That is a bit weird."

"Very, if you ask me."

"Anything else?"

"Well one of his bookmarked websites is an unsolved crime site. I checked it out and the crimes that are discussed are brutal. Not the famous stuff like who killed JonBenét Ramsey and some others that I never heard of. Some of the crimes involve grisly killings. Several are parental murders. I have to confess that I found a certain fascination reading some of the stories, repulsive though they were. That said, I can't see myself searching them out and bookmarking the page. Grace, I think you had a real weirdo working for you."

"Do you think that makes him a weirdo? There used to be a TV show called "Unsolved Mysteries." It ran for years and was really popular. People just seem to like that sort of thing."

"Grace, the page was bookmarked. It's not like on a whim he just wanted to check it out. He bookmarked the site. Plus he wants to date old women."

"Careful, little buddy."

Jenny knew she had inserted her foot squarely into her mouth but was quick to see the escape route. "Grace, the reason he didn't hit on you is that you're too young."

"Well, that was an adept recovery."

∞

The following day, Jenny showed Grace some of the personal stuff that Roscoe had left on the Lenovo. She went from site to site with minimal commentary.

"I must say," Grace allowed, "you really have discovered some things about Roscoe that I wouldn't have imagined. But you know, if the guy just wanted to disappear for some reason, doesn't it make sense that he would want to read about unsolved crimes. I have to believe that every one of them involves the disappearance of the guy who did it. Maybe the descriptions tell some of the ways that people can disappear.

"Anyway, Jenny, I'm beginning to think that I can put Roscoe out of my mind. I haven't heard anything from or about him. I haven't heard from any pesticide company telling me to shut down or they'll kill me. My thought is that we should just put the whole thing behind us and move on. You seem to like your job. Let's carry on with what we're doing."

"Sorry to say, you're wrong this time, Grace. This is a mystery. Nobody seems to give a damn. The cops don't care, neither here nor in The Dalles. The Corps of Engineers rubber stamped a permit that's full of discrepancies. Something's going on. We need to figure out what it is. Grace, I need to earn that tattoo."

"Okay, I'll make you a deal. If we hear anything that we think might help us find Roscoe, or figure out what he's up to, we'll pursue it. But we can't take time away from work to chase after a shadow. We need something solid to go on. At this point the only way we're going to get that is if we hear about it – meaning someone tells us, or we read about it somewhere."

CHAPTER TWENTY-SIX

Roscoe lay on his back peering up at the stars through the partly broken window in his cabin. Because it was clear, he knew the night would be cold, but he felt pleased with the progress that had been made over the last couple of weeks on his wild rice facilities.

As he listened to the usual after-dark sounds of rodents scampering about inside his cabin, he found himself thinking back to two particularly exciting nights four years ago. He had learned on his visit to the two Columbia River salmon hatcheries, that the salmon smolts from that year were to be released over a several day period the following month. At the time of his visit the smolts were being held in designated raceways. Roscoe had marveled at the density of fish that were crowded into the raceways. Soon they would be free of this miserable life they've had, he thought. They will swim downstream into the ocean and have no bounds to where they can go. Some will die, he realized from his reading. They would die from predation, or being caught in the great run-of-the-river turbines at The Dalles and Bonneville. Some would die of gas embolisms after being swept over the spillway. Some would be swept into irrigation diversions. Some would die of diseases contracted in the hatchery, and many will be just too weak genetically to survive the rigors of the migration from freshwater to seawater. After reaching the ocean, more would be caught by sport fishermen and commercial fishermen trolling for salmon.

But many, he knew, would survive the migration and live at sea until they felt the urge to return and spawn. What triggered that urge, he wondered. He knew that their life in the ocean could be from one to six or even seven years, but that most would return in four years. Then they would face other hazards as they began their upstream migration. Some would wind up in the permit regulated gill net fishery of the American Indian tribes on the Columbia. It is a perilous life that salmon lead. In his mind's eye, he reviewed photographs and videos he had seen of the indomitable silvery Chinooks ascending arduous barriers. Remarkable, indeed, that they have survived in spite of the habitat destruction and hazards that humans have placed in their paths. What's one more peril? I'm but one man. These fish have survived in spite of the abuses of civilization – channelization, flood control, shipping traffic, power generation, pollution, and sophisticated inventions such as fish wheels and nets of all descriptions to harvest them.

I, myself, am a survivor, he thought. If I were a salmon, I would be one who made it back to my natal stream and spawned. Whatever I might do to tempt any individual fish, others will swim on.

I can do whatever I damn please, Roscoe said to himself as he contemplated adding one more impediment to the long list. His plan would be just one more thing that would separate the stupid salmon from the smart ones. If there are already ten hurdles, what's another, he thought. The salmon that are tough and smart are magnificent. They can leap great waterfalls. In Alaska they swim past brown bears capable of snagging them out of the air as they leap falls and rapids. My own little experiment won't be much of a problem for such an imposing creature.

8

On the two particular nights that found their way into his conscious thought, Roscoe had returned to the hatcheries – one each night. He found both facilities heavily guarded by fencing, floodlighting, and night patrolling guards. These efforts to discourage unauthorized intrusion proved to be only minor nuisances to Roscoe. Upon arriving, he watched the movement of the guards from a spot where shadows hid him from view. He counted out the time intervals that the guards were out of the direct sight line from his destination as they made their rounds of the hatchery. When he had assured himself of the regularity of their routine, he climbed the fence, clipped the razor wire on the top and let himself down on the other side. He looked at his watch and it had taken him a minute longer than he estimated. Not to worry. He still had two minutes to run to the smolt raceways, empty his vials into the water, and run back to his point of entry. The procedure was exciting, but glitch free at both hatcheries.

He watched the websites of both facilities for a couple of weeks, but there was never any mention of a break in. He actually wondered if they had failed to discover the snipped razor wire, but he didn't need to know. His mission had been completed successfully.

Roscoe Toth lay quietly, as the creatures of the night made themselves at home in his hillside lair. Things were falling into place. Tomorrow night he would carry out the next step of his magnificent scheme.

CHAPTER TWENTY-SEVEN

It became an effort for Jenny to keep her mind on her work at the lab. Even though Grace encouraged her and said that the production process was close at hand, Jenny kept thinking about what she had found on Roscoe's computer. Much of what she did for Jenny required full focus on the task. She had to force Roscoe out of her mind at least until lunchtime, when she usually spent a half hour to an hour eating and contemplating the coincidences that she had condensed to three: Roscoe's strange disappearance; the fact that his biological father was probably murdered; and the fact that Roscoe was reading about unsolved crimes on the internet.

Could he be trying to solve the mystery of his father's disappearance? Not likely, she thought. The man had been missing for ten years. During that time Roscoe had started and finished a difficult major at Cal and had worked for Grace for three or four years – Jenny wasn't sure how long, but it didn't matter. The key number was ten.

Could he have killed his own father? He had been a suspect at the time, but he was something like fourteen years old. It didn't seem likely. What would his motive have been? Even if you hypothesized that he did it, what would be the reason he would suddenly disappear now? Nope, that does not appear to fit. Maybe he did, but probably he didn't. The important fact is still that Roscoe is missing and could be dead himself. Jenny thought about that possibility. No, no, no, she thought. Murdered by a big pesticide company? No way, that's a story that the guy made up, but why?

Jenny reviewed the coincidences and facts again. Her thought process was organized as carefully as if she were parsing a sentence. Her father would approve. Finally, without any new information or supportive evidence she said to herself, *Roscoe is in Dufur.* She wanted to tell Grace what she had concluded, but it was the same old story – speculation based on sketchy information.

∓

Grace sat at her own desk eating the chicken sandwich that Jenny had made that morning. She had been thinking about Roscoe for the last twenty minutes almost unconsciously. There was no sorting or organization of information in her thoughts, nor was she driving toward a conclusion. More accurately, she was in a state of idle curiosity. This was not a rare occurrence. Even though she had told Jenny to forget about Roscoe, she hadn't been able to do that herself.

As she sat in a daze, her phone rang causing her to start. "Hello?"

Jenny listened to the half of the conversation that she could hear. Grace had blanched as the conversation began.

"Oh, my god."

"No."

"Oh, my god."

"Oh, good grief. What a relief."

The conversation continued with only brief responses from Grace and Jenny began to sense fear that there really was a hit man, and he'd found Grace.

As soon as Grace placed the phone back in its charger, Jenny turned the back of her chair to Grace's desk and shoved so hard with her feet that she rolled directly to a spot adjacent to Grace's desk. "What in the world was that?"

"It was a major scare, at first. But it turned out to be nothing."

"Well? What happened?"

"It was a guy who said he represented a pesticide company. That's when I almost lost it. But as the conversation unfolded, it turned out that they had read all of my press releases and wanted to discuss a collaboration or even a merger."

"What did you tell him?"

"That I wasn't interested. I took his name though, because I might be at some future time."

"Good for you. Why did you even take his name?"

"Money's tight, Jenny. Plus this outfit would have all the facilities we would need to manufacture on a full-production scale, they have all the distribution systems in place, all the markets and wholesalers and final users identified. The Graceful Death could go ballistic over night."

"Now you make it sound like you should have considered the offer."

"That's the trouble. He wouldn't give me a figure. He just wanted to talk. No offer. I could call any of a half dozen companies and offer to talk, and they would all jump at the chance. I told the guy that if they were thinking of collaboration or merger, they needed to throw me a ballpark figure."

"What do you think that would be?"

"At this very moment, probably twenty mil."

"Million? God, Grace, you could retire and play tennis all the time. You could build you own tennis court."

"Jenny, in a month, if you keep your analyses and trial runs going, and I keep my research on track, the value of what we have will be a hundred times that. The pesticide market is enormous. To be honest, I see the future of my company as a division of some large corporation. When it happens, they'll offer me some job in their research and development division where I'd answer to some suave suit who was so masterful at the art of cliché that he would be able to say nothing and make it sound good."

"That sounds bad, Grace."

"At that point I would tell them thanks but no thanks. I'll tell them that this is not a merger, it's an outright sale, and if they need me, I'll be at the construction site of my new tennis court."

"You're so clever, Grace. And I'll be solving crimes for Interpol."

"Not unless you want to."

"What's that supposed to mean?"

"It means that if you work for me until something like that happens, and if you get your degree at Cal, that you will get a little of this windfall for yourself. I don't have any kids, Jenny. How am I going to spend a zillion dollars?"

Jenny could not believe she wasn't dreaming. She looked around for clues that she was in a real life situation, and decided she was, but she couldn't think of anything to say. Finally, she said, "Well, Grace, I'm glad it wasn't a death threat."

෨

Jenny finally found the right words to express her gratitude. She started with the ride to Berkeley, the invitation to occupy the guestroom, the job and everything else, right up to this incredible offer to share the wealth that seemed destined to come her way. She didn't say it, but Jenny realized that Roscoe had very likely walked away from the same sort of an offer. The offer was vague, but Jenny knew Grace well enough to be sure that her offer wasn't a spur of the moment whim. She had already thought it through.

"I'm very hesitant to bring Roscoe into this conversation, Grace, but I think your call could be considered a data point."

"Huh?"

"Sorry, my dad always referred to incoming information as data points."

"Well, you're right. It was a data point."

"Here's what I mean. Isn't a call like that the kind of thing that you would expect a corporation to do if they saw your press releases and became worried about their ability to compete? I mean that kind of approach is what would happen. A death threat to the lab tech is not what would happen."

"So how does that bear on anything?"

"What it tells me is that our intuition about Roscoe being alive and in hiding is probably correct. It's just one more thing that suggests that he did not get the death threat that he told you about. My guess is that he got no call of any kind, and that he had something in mind that was not only secret, but was very urgent. And extrapolating that one step further, whatever that might have been, he's doing it now. I still want to know what that is."

"Jenny, you have to do it on your own time. We're on the cusp of something pretty huge right now. You have to stick with me. I essentially offer you a share of this growing opportunity, and you still focus on Roscoe. Get over it."

"You're right. I'll try. But I'm an aspiring detective, Grace. It's not going to be easy."

৪০

Grace's phone rang again. Before picking it up, she asked Jenny to run a couple of new samples through the gas chromatograph and bring her the printout.

CHAPTER TWENTY-EIGHT

As originally designed, the effluent canal from the wild rice building would have required six truck-loads of redi-mix concrete. Roscoe's change order had reduced that to one truck which poured foundations for the piers that supported the wooden flume. The job foreman at the Jepson ranch had been successful in canceling the delivery, but in the process had lost the trust of one of his suppliers. When he started to lecture Roscoe about that, the next time he saw him, Roscoe walked away gesturing back to him as he did so. It took every bit of constraint that the foreman could muster not to teach the boy something about the combat moves he had learned as a Navy Seal. The following day the foreman contacted Larry Jepson to tell him he was on the verge of walking off the job with the whole construction crew.

Jepson had a hunch that Roscoe was lurking around and living in the rat hole on the hill, but had not been aware that he was monkeying around with the project design. The wild rice production idea had been Roscoe's in the first place, so Jepson had cut Roscoe some slack in managing the project. But he did not like what he heard from the contractor.

"Margo," he said one evening, "that kid of yours is up to something, and I don't know what it is. This wild rice idea of his don't make sense. I don't doubt that you have to freeze the seed, but after that you have to grow the stuff. Where the hell is he going to do that? There's no place on this whole spread where you can flood a paddy."

"Oh, Larry, Roscoe is so excited about this idea of his. You know he needs to succeed at something. He's the smartest kid in Dufur, but except for what he's done in school here and at the university down in Berkeley, he's been aimless. The poor boy is bouncing around like a pinball. Maybe we should just let him do his thing."

"His *thing* is costing a fortune. I'm about to pull the plug on his *thing*. Plus, why is the guy so furtive about everything. That kid needs his ass whipped, if you ask me. Livin' up there with all them creatures and their filth, that's not normal. I know we agreed not to talk about this, but are you absolutely sure that he didn't have anything to do with Joe's disappearance?"

"Larry. Stop it. You're damn right we agreed not to talk about that. The police have already looked into it. How do I know that *you* didn't have something to do with it?"

"I've about had it with your son, Margo. I don't know how much longer I can let him keep on with this fly-brained scheme of his."

∞

Margo had told Roscoe of Larry's objections to Roscoe's life style, and whatever else it was that he was doing, which Larry doubted had anything to do with wild rice; but Roscoe assured her that everything would be all right. He told her he had a surprise in mind that would amaze them.

In spite of his assurance to his mother, Roscoe had one misgiving that he had to overcome. Up until now he had been able to carry out all his plans using the job crew and the massive amounts of equipment that could be found in the outbuildings around the wheat ranch. Now he needed a certain item to complete his project and in order to get it he needed to make a trip to The Dalles.

ɞ

Not many people in The Dalles knew Ross Jepson. He had never played any sport in high school. He had never even attempted to get on a sailboard. And he had by his own reverence to his mother, earned her overindulgence. In other words, he was spoiled, knew it, and thought of it as one of his virtues. Whenever Roscoe needed something, he got it by asking his mother to get it for him. Thus, Mrs. Jepson was known around town, but Roscoe wasn't. In fact Mrs. Jepson was well known around town, and thrived on the attention she received.

The Dalles, Oregon is not known for its lively night life. People have been known to say such things as that they roll up the sidewalks at seven o'clock. Roscoe was aware of this and planed his trip to the big city for seven-thirty. He knew that the Gucci store stayed open until eight. In the dark of the winter night, he rode his 50cc Honda to town on a side road and requested the needed item at the store. He knew exactly what he wanted, and became agitated when the sales lady discussed other options. The little episode with this woman caused him to have difficulty starting up his Honda, as in his haste to get away he flooded it. Finally, after waiting several minutes for it to clear, he got it started and rode off in the darkness, still feeling angry.

Nevertheless, by the time he got back to his lair, he felt confident that he'd been unseen. It had been dark. He wore a baseball cap with no logo of any kind, and he'd worn a long wool overcoat. Back at his hideaway he had that triumphant feeling that he had felt so often in his life, starting with the nights when during his grammar school years he would crawl into his mother's bed.

ɞ

When Grace picked up the phone, the voice on the other end said, "Ms. Summers, this is Lem. Remember me? Lem Russell from The Dalles?"

CHAPTER TWENTY-NINE

On the previous Friday Grace had given Jenny a ride down to
Telegraph Avenue so she could visit the book stores, and also
talk to someone in the registrar's office about delaying her
admission. Jenny bought a course catalog and was disappointed to discover that in her first year she would not be taking any criminology courses. There was a sociology course
that sounded appealing, but the criminology courses required
in the major were not offered until upper division. The store
owner had a copy of the books required for many of the courses, and Jenny purchased a used copy of a book on the development of criminal personalities.

"Why in the world would you want to do that?" Grace inquired. "You won't need that until at least two years from
now, and who knows whether they'll be using the same
book."

"I just want to get a feeling for the educational aspects of
looking at crime. Here we are in the midst of an intriguing
mystery, and maybe it's just the excitement that keys my interest in criminology. Maybe when I'm learning the workings
of the trade I won't be so excited."

"Seems reasonable," Grace said, at the same time wanting
to remind Jenny that they were no longer in pursuit of the
elusive Mr. Toth.

"Hey," Jenny said, "too bad that Roscoe's name isn't
Waldo. We'd be part of a real live 'Where's Waldo' adventure."

Jenny's thought process was usually so organized that Grace often forgot that she was only seventeen years old. The Waldo comment reminded her that there was still a child in that body.

Jenny went on. "Can you imagine how boring it would be to write the 'Where's Waldo' books. Imagine drawing around a thousand pictures that all looked exactly alike except that one of em wore glasses. The guy who wrote those books must have escaped from the bin."

"Wouldn't you guess that the people who read those books might also be bin dwellers?"

"No. Absolutely not. They're kids. It's criminology for kids."

"Page after page? Book after book?"

"Yep. You gotta remember what it's like to be a kid."

"I guess you're right. Where do you suppose Roscoe is right now?"

"Dufur. Dufer, Oregon. Ninety-three percent. Six percent, somewhere else in the world. One percent, dead."

∞

Although the name Lem Russell had a familiar ring, it took her several seconds to remember who he was. She was thankful that he'd mentioned The Dalles. "Well, hi, Lem. What occasions the pleasure of hearing from you?"

"Afternoon, ma'am, you're asking why I'm calling, right?"

"Yes, I wanted you to know that it's nice to hear from you. What's up?"

"I thought you might want to know that I spotted Ross Jepson here in town last night. I remembered you'd been asking about him, so I thought it would be the right thing to do to give you a call."

"You saw him last night in The Dalles?"

"Yes, I did."

"What was he doing?"

161

"Well when I saw him he was trying to get his little Honda fired up. At first he wasn't having much luck. I was going to tell him to pull the plug, but it looked to me that he was kind of in incognito mode, you might say."

"It appeared to you that he didn't want to be recognized?"

"That's right. That's how it appeared."

"Where was he?"

"Now that's the strange part. He was in front of the Gucci store. I doubt you've been up here enough to know it, but the Gucci store is exclusive. I would be confident to say there's not much in there that would attract or appeal to a farm boy. They do have some stuff for men, but it's fancy Italian stuff from Italy."

"You're right that I haven't been to The Dalles Gucci shop, but what you say is pretty much true of all of them."

"Well, yeah, it's like I say. Not much in there that a farm boy would be looking for. That's the main reason I didn't help him get his Honda started. See, I figured the guy was in there for some reason or other that was embarrassing to him. That's why he was in his incognito suit. I just said to myself, 'Lem, leave him alone.'"

"This is all very interesting. Anything else?"

"Whatever he got wasn't big. I think he had a little bag in his hand. One of those little white bags with string handles. Like I said, he had trouble getting underway, but when he did, he took one of the back roads to Dufur that isn't the main one." Lem suddenly started laughing. "Cotton pick," he said. "What was that boy doing in a Gucci shop. I wonder if old man Jepson knows about that."

"Well, Lem, many thanks for your call. Remember when we were there we thought he might have been murdered. You sensed then that it was just a missing person situation. So out of two missing Toths, you found one. That's better than zero, I guess." As soon as Grace had said that she wished she hadn't. It sounded more adolescent than Jenny.

"Heh,heh. I guess you're right. One find is better than zero. That's a good one. Okay, Grace. I'll keep you posted if I hear anything."

Again, Jenny rolled her chair across the room to Grace's desk. "If I heard what I think I heard, Roscoe is alive and living in Dufur, Oregon. Am I right?"

"Right you are, Jen."

"So what did you find out?"

"That Ross shops at Gucci." Grace went on to tell Jenny the details of her conversation with Lem.

I wonder why Roscoe would go to the Gucci shop. He advertised that he was interested in older women. Maybe he got himself a date and wanted to get her a Gucci something or other."

"Lem said he was dressed weird. Incognito mode, he called it."

"Grace, there's something about you that I just can not understand."

"What's that?"

"Why did you like this man?"

"He's smart. And when he worked for me, he got the jobs done. As I told you, he took his time outs, but he was good at the tasks you've been doing. I could count on him most of the time."

"And now he's up to something, Grace. If he's that smart, whatever he's up to is not simplistic. Now we know he's alive and we know where he is. Very likely, he's still hiding out because he's only been sighted once, and he was in incognito mode. So now we move on to *why and what?* Why is he hiding? And what is he up to?"

"We're not moving on, Jen. We're going to stay right where we are and say, '*Well, I'll be*' and let it go at that. Evidently his life is not in danger. That being the case, neither is mine. You've got a job. If you stay with me and you complete your degree in criminology, you get a share of the profits. My take on life at this moment is that it's pretty good. Let's not do something that might rock the boat."

"I wouldn't be honest if I didn't tell you I was disappointed. But I'm stuck. You've got the car. If you're not interested in solving this mystery there's just not one thing I can do about it."

Grace felt a pang of guilt. She knew that Jenny was juiced by the mystery surrounding Roscoe's disappearance, as even she herself was to some degree. But they now knew what they had set out to learn. Roscoe was alive. "You're right, Jen. You're stuck."

"How about agreeing that if we hear anything else, we'll resume our investigation. I mean especially if it's something kind of weird."

"Okay. I will be the judge of whether it's weird."

"Deal. Thanks, Gracie."

CHAPTER THIRTY

The natural tendency upon creating a masterpiece is to want to show it to someone. Roscoe wondered if his distant ancestor Lazlo had considered his attack of the Pietà in the Sistine Chapel a masterful accomplishment. Probably not. The guy was bonkers. He thought he was Jesus Christ for god's sake. Plus there was no waiting involved. Instant gratification because there were a bunch of people there watching when he did it. The guy was judged to be insane and was never punished. Roscoe contemplated what insanity must feel like. Could he, himself, be insane? He felt as normal as a bell curve. But then he wondered if thinking of that particular analog to normality made him abnormal.

Roscoe had a couple more details to finish on his carefully planned project. Then he would have to bide time for at least four weeks, before applying the final "brush stroke." He had not yet decided whether or not to be present when the curtain was raised for the final act. There were advantages to being absent, but he doubted he would be able to stay away from his grand experiment. Only time would tell, for careful timing was essential to success.

Larry and Margo had an engagement to join friends in The Dalles at Baldwin's Saloon, one of their favorite dinner spots. They were regular patrons, and Roscoe knew that once they left the ranch they were certain to be gone for four hours or more. It was always a festive evening for them and their friends, and they always made it last. Although he had plenty of time to put the finishing touches on his project, he decided that he might as well do it that evening while Larry and his mother were gone. By doing that he left plenty of time to review some of the information that he needed to complete the undertaking successfully.

Underneath the flooring of his little cabin was the final element needed to carry out his plan. It was fragile and Roscoe had worried over how he could get it to the construction site. But over time, he drew a plan for a transporter that he would be able to carry on his Honda. With extreme caution and moving slowly and surely, he had the carrier and its contents affixed to the Honda securely. By the time it was in position, two and a half hours had passed. He felt a little pressure, but at this point there was no turning back. He drove the Honda slowly down the rutted road to the place where the new flume had been built adjoining the dam that held his settling pond. There were places along the path of the flume where it was elevated above the ground by several inches. Roscoe had excavated one of these spots to enlarge the opening, and had marked the spot with a steel fence post several days previously. When he got to where he thought the marker was, he couldn't find it. After a search, he discovered the hole where it had been. Clearly someone had got rid of it. Not a problem, he thought, but it had cost him another ten minutes. He set the Honda on its stand and carefully removed the carrier. With all the care that he could summon, he slid the carrier into the opening that he had created and with a shovel, back filled it so that the ground level touched the bottom of the flume. Then with haste but meticulous care, he covered his tracks in the soil, the disturbances in the earth that he had made around the flume, and the hole where he had placed the steel post. The Honda tire marks extended only a short distance from hard ground and he smoothed them with the shovel. In all he had taken four and a half hours for the task, but the senior Jepsons had not yet returned.

At that moment, however, he saw the car headlights undulating in the air, as their car navigated the road down to the ranch house. Roscoe started the Honda and without turning on his own headlight gunned it up the hill toward the house where his road intersected the driveway. Seconds before the car lights shown upon him he swerved onto his own road and was out of sight as the car arrived.

Back in the safety of his cabin, his breath came in dog-like pants and he could feel his heart beating in his chest. Close calls make life exhilarating, he thought. Stealthily, he replaced the flooring that he'd removed and kicked some debris and droppings around to camouflage the work area.

When he got into his down bedroll his breathing and heartbeat had returned to normal. He felt the sense of accomplishment that came with knowing that all his planning and care was about to yield grand results. About four more weeks should do it. He could not wait.

CHAPTER THIRTY-ONE

As weeks passed, Jenny became more agitated about the absence of any further information about Roscoe. In her mind there was little doubt that Roscoe was up to something and whatever it was, it was evil. In her spare time she looked at old outlines of her thought train, and made new ones. Now that they knew he was alive and in The Dalles or Dufur, the choices were much diminished. As clues dried up, her obsession grew. Her latest analytical chart was titled *What's He Doing?* Beneath that she had two choices: A. Something Good; and B. Something Bad. She was not able to parse those choices, so she wrote short narrative statements. Under A, she wrote, "If he is doing something good, why would he have disappeared, and why would he have stayed in hiding." The only answer was that he really did get a death threat and he was making it hard for someone, whoever made it, to carry it out. She wrote, "Death threat real; hiding out to avoid getting killed."

Jenny could not reconcile that choice. If it was true, all the clues and intuition that led them to believe he was up to something fell out of consideration. That possibility just did not make sense. She felt that if she could get up to Dufur somehow and snoop around, she very well might discover something that would shed some light on her thought process. The other thing she wanted to do was brainstorm the clues with Grace, but Grace was steadfastly against even talking about Roscoe. *Here this woman brings a mystery into my life and now she won't even talk about it,* Jenny thought.

To her credit she did not bug Grace. She respected Grace's position and still felt overwhelming gratitude for all that Grace had done for her. She also liked the job, and they were making progress.

Jenny's day to day tasks were analyzing the chemical composition of pheromones that were produced under different conditions. For example, by putting spiders into the same cage as pest insects, the insects would produce a fear pheromone that would cause others of that species to be repulsed. The different conditions that Grace set up to stimulate pheromone production were fascinating. Jenny had become an expert at operating the analytical equipment. Meanwhile, Grace was working on reconstituting the compounds in mass quantities. She had been successful on a couple of them, and had developed the techniques involved to the point where she was on the doorstep of achieving a standardized technique.

The one thing that Grace had consistently said about Roscoe was that he was smart. He had to have known how close Grace was to a remedy for insect depredation – perhaps the single most destructive aspect of crop production. Jenny had no way to estimate how much global food supplies would increase, but it would be a lot. She thought back to Jeff the Okie talking about foxes and rabbits. There is no doubt that Roscoe knew that Grace was onto something huge, but he quit anyway. Why? The book Jenny had bought from the bookstore on Telegraph Avenue had several chapters that discussed personality disorders that correlated to criminal behavior. Jenny had read and reread the chapters and the only thing it did for her was make her aware of the possibility that Roscoe, in spite of being smart, had some kind of a disorder that guided him to make irrational decisions. But where did that get her? Nowhere. She had never met the guy. And even if she had, she wouldn't have been able to discern something about him that Grace had never noticed.

Without telling Grace, Jenny subscribed to the online edition of The Dalles Chronicle. She read it every morning either on her iPhone or on her laptop at work. It was now early March and nothing, to date had been written about Roscoe. While Jenny's interest level remained high, her optimism waned. She began to see why police investigations went cold. What can you do when there are no additional data points? All you can do is wonder.

ॐ

The Ides of March, thought Roscoe. Wasn't that one of those days that would live in infamy? The day Julius Caesar was assassinated by four men that he trusted? What an absurd belief trust is. Self confidence? Yes. Confidence in others? Nay.

In two weeks, on the ides of March, Roscoe would start a domino effect of events. It was hard for him to believe it would work, but from what he had learned from Grace and from Missy, he had to have confidence. There it was, confidence, another kind of trust. But not in a person. In an expectation based on the known consistency of certain kinds of events. The sun always rises in the east.

All systems go, he thought. Where did those words come from? Then it came to him. That's what they say when they're about to launch a space craft. Who says it? The guy inside the shuttle? Or was it someone in the Houston Space Center? How in the world does the guy who says it know that it's true. *Can that person be trusted,* he wondered. Well, what Roscoe was about to do was just as significant as launching a space vehicle. Then after a moment of thought he said quietly to himself, "Not." But it *was* an event that would be noticed. No doubt about that.

Other than getting good grades, Roscoe had never done anything significant. The thought that he was about to cause some level of curiosity in his community excited him. He still had his doubts about how things would play out, but isn't that always true of even the simplest plan? He believed that he had anticipated most of the possibilities for failure and made his plans accordingly. He realized that failure was a possibility, but as he reviewed the set up, he was pretty sure that it wouldn't be his fault. In fact the only source of failure that he could think of now was that he might have misinterpreted something that he learned. Either that or something that he learned was not true and never had been. Considering the sources, he had to think that was unlikely. From now until the ides, I count the days, he thought.

CHAPTER THIRTY-TWO

Deanna Rivera was in her sixth year as a fish counter at the John Day Dam fishway. By the end of her first week she was ninety-nine percent accurate in identifying the species of fish that flashed by the counting window. For many it would have been a tedious job, but she loved it, was good at what she did, and had received recognition for it. Her guidance came from FPOM, the Fish Passage Operations and Management Committee. FPOM, in turn, consisted of biologists from NOAA, CRITFC, ODFW, WDFW, IDFW, BPA, and COE, an alphabet soup of agencies that struggled to find ways to accomplish goals unique to their own charters, and at the same time accomplish shared goals. One of the shared goals was for Deanna to report large numbers as she counted the salmon runs. Historically, there were seasonal fluctuations based on runoff and other factors, but ever since construction of the many dams on the Columbia River and its tributaries had begun, the counts of upstream migrant salmon had been less than robust with a decisive downward trend. Over the years, countless staff-hours had gone into attempting to protect the runs. Some efforts were called mitigation and some were called enhancement. None achieved the goals of improving what nature herself had accomplished.

Salmon spawn in the fall, but the runs are identified by the time of year they enter the river for their spawning migration. The spring run fish historically ran far upstream – so far that they did not arrive at their spawning destination until it was time to spawn in the fall. They were characteristically huge Chinook salmon in peak condition, prepared to swim more than a thousand miles without feeding. There were waterfalls to ascend, predators to avoid, and many other perils ever present on their great final journey to spawn. Early efforts to restore the runs centered on hatchery production. Although there is evidence that hatchery reared fish have weakened the populations over the years, it is still one of the primary tools that managers rely on. Procedures have been modified to try to eliminate the factors that have weakened the gene pool. But the fact remains that most of the fish that now go to sea never had to survive the perils of natural spawning that their ancestors did. As those ancestral combatants become more and more distant in their contribution to the genetic structure of the Chinook salmon populations, the inevitable result is deterioration of the health of the returning stocks.

Deanna had attended a class or two taught by a field biologist from the Portland District office of the Corps of Engineers. But the shortcomings and failings of the efforts to keep the Chinook runs healthy were never mentioned. The emphasis was on how to instantly identify the twelve or so different species that would swim past her window – some nearly identical in appearance – and Deanna mastered it. It was a worthy cause, of course. The counts are a major contributor to the scientific management programs that function to keep the multi-billion dollar salmon industries viable.

Deanna's sister, Angie, held the job as fish counter at The Dalles Dam, about thirty miles downstream from Deanna's station. At a ninety-seven percent accuracy level, she did not get as many rewards as her sister, but she was better looking than Deanna and had a better social life, so she experienced no envy of her sister's job achievements. Indeed, she felt a little sorry for her. But they were close and lived together in Hood River, one of the world's great sailboarding meccas. The jobs of both women required full attention so they could not talk on the phone, send text messages or have any other distractions. Both were night counters. They sat in a dank subterranean vault with a lighted window in front of them where fish flash by as they ascended the ladders. Not only did they make instant identification of species, but also if they were early returners – jacks as they were called – and whether they were fin-clipped or not. During the peak of the runs their fingers would fly over the keys of the counting machines as if they were in a typing speed test. Each was allowed several breaks during the night, and it was on those breaks that they occasionally would communicate.

&

The interior of Roscoe's wild rice freezing facility consisted of four General Electric multi-shelf freezers. The shelves, each with it's own refrigeration coil, were six inches apart. There were several five-horsepower garbage disposers and an array of cutting tables with laminated hardwood tops. A water supply line from the irrigation system was attached to the intake of a 150-horsepower electric pump running on 480 volts. The water output was five cubic feet per second into a two thousand gallon tank. That discharged into the settling pond just riverward of the building, then into the covered wooden flume that carried it to the Deschutes River, and then to the Columbia. The flume was four feet high from floor to cover with built-in eighteen inch weirs that kept the flow velocity fairly constant. Roscoe estimated the weir positions without any background in hydraulic engineering, but he trusted his placement based on what he had read in a book called *Shape and Flow.*

&

"What in the hell is Ross doing down there?" Larry asked Margo in exasperation. "He's up to something that has nothing to do with wild rice. Have you been in that building of his?"

"Lord, no. Why in the world would I ever go down there. All that stuff you boys do is foreign to me. Mercy. I'm afraid to leave the house unless you're with me – all that equipment that's always driving around. Don't you guys ever stop?"

"I know what I'm doing, Margo, but I don't know what the hell your kid is up to. You need to talk to him."

"*I need to?* I wouldn't know what to say. If he needs talking to, you're the one that needs to do it. If you took me down to his building and gave me a tour, I still wouldn't know what the hell you were showing me. *You talk to him.*"

"Okay, let's say I agree to talk to him. *How can I do it when he's hiding up there in that vermin nest?* Margo, I know you hate it when I say this, but there's something amiss in the attic with that boy."

"He's smart. Leave him alone."

That ended the conversation between Margo and Larry Jepson on March 14th. They had had similar discussions before and the outcome was almost always the same.

Tomorrow was the ides of March, a day that meant nothing to either Margo or Larry Jepson. Both had read Shakespeare's *Julius Caesar* during their high school years, but neither remembered anything about the ides.

CHAPTER THIRTY-THREE

The following night, Roscoe drove his Honda slowly down the hill to his new facility. It was ten o'clock and the moon provided enough ambient light so that he did not need to turn on the headlamp. The building was cold inside. Heating was supplied by a 240 volt overhead electric unit with a large fan that circulated warm air. It was inadequate in the cavernous building, but it took the bite out of the chill.

With a feeling of excitement and anticipation, Roscoe opened the valve to his pump inlet and started the pump, which shot water into the two thousand gallon tank. The tank was full in less than a minute and water began flowing into the settling pond, which filled in twenty minutes, thence down the laddered flume to the Deschutes and Columbia Rivers. Roscoe's excitement grew as he toured the building and confirmed that everything was working as it was supposed to. All systems go, he thought, smiling with self satisfaction. He waited through the night for the first fish to appear, spending much of the time on the low dam, watching the outlet through an opening in the top of the flume. Shortly before dawn, feeling deflated and impotent, he shut down the pump and returned to his den. His million dollar project had failed. He sat on the edge of his cot pondering the reason.

It did not take Roscoe long to figure out what had gone wrong. In his excitement, his focus had been on whether his hydraulic design would work. That had been the weak link in his planning – the part where he had made guesses when he should have consulted engineers. But he could trust no one to that task. He lived by the old adage that three can keep a secret if two of them are dead. Although he could not see what was happening in the flume he believed it must be working right because no water backed up into the building and the flume held together. So if it wasn't a hydraulic problem, it could have been either of two things. He knew at the outset that he might be early for the spring run. There was always some variation in the onset, but it had been a wet winter and the Columbia flow was high. Those conditions usually led to early onset of the run. Suddenly he laughed at himself when he realized that after four years of careful planning he had forgotten the most essential ingredient in the recipe – the Gucci *Guilty Absolute Eau de Parfum.*

Four years previously, Roscoe had thrown the contents of several vials of the stuff into the smolt raceways at the Bonneville and Oxbow salmon hatcheries. He knew from his course in ichthyology that the smolts would imprint on the smell and would bust their tails to get back to a place that smelled the same when they made their spawning run. The discovery that olfactory cues were the final navigation input to their natal spawning riffle is what had given Roscoe the idea to guide the run into his own processing plant. All he needed to do was imprint the fish at the time they were released as smolts, or downstream migrants, and then after growing for four years in the food-rich waters of the Eastern Pacific, they would find their way into the mouth of the Columbia River and start their upstream migration. Driven to find their natal spawning ground, they would begin to sniff their way upstream until they found that imprinted scent – *Guilty Absolute Eau de Parfum.* But in his excitement and haste to get started, Roscoe had forgotten the scent that would lure them to their "home." He had forgotten the *Guilty Absolute Eau de Parfum.*

He did not forget it the next night. Inside his processing building he had a medical IV arrangement that he had set up so that it would drip once each hour into the two thousand gallon tank. The amount was minute, he knew, but it was based on literature that he had read while working for Grace Summers about the sensing abilities of various organisms. The olfactory sense of salmon to detect minuscule concentrations of water-soluble compounds was legendary and well documented. No human, not Gucci himself, could ever smell *parfum* in the attraction flow emerging from his flume.

That night as he moved back and forth from inside the building to the crest of his small dam, he saw the first evidence that his plan was going to succeed. Two silvery forms entered the pond and from there quickly jumped the cascade of water over a low barrier into the interior tank. Roscoe dressed the two Chinooks and placed them on one of the freezer shelves.

During ensuing days he caught two to four fish each night until the twelfth night when sixty-eight fish leaped into his tank. *We are in a Shakespearean rhythm*, he thought.

That night, Roscoe dressed all of the fish, and set electric timers to operate the pumps and I.V. drip so that in his absence, the facility would continue to operate only at night. He then mounted his Honda and headed across the Great River of the West *en route* to Canada. It would be a slow trip on the tiny vehicle, but he didn't care. There was more to his project than catching salmon.

CHAPTER THIRTY-FOUR

On the night that Roscoe's salmon highjacking scheme hit its high mark of sixty-eight fish, Larry Jepson was awakened by the sound of running water. Peering out of his bedroom window, he could see threads of light reaching out through the small windows in the rice freezing building. He woke Margo. "Ross is doing something down in the building."

Half asleep, Margo said, "What?"

"How should I know? I can see the lights are on and I can hear water running. How am I supposed to know what he's doing?"

"Maybe you should check it out. Don't do it now, though, wait until tomorrow. Just get back in bed. It'll wait."

In Larry's mind it was good advice, so he crawled back into bed mumbling something that sounded like, "God damn kid."

When Larry awoke the next morning, he went down to the building and inspected the unusual interior design, including the elaborate water system which stumped him. He still wasn't sure what he was looking at, but he knew it had nothing to do with wild rice. He found the salmon in the freezer but didn't know where they came from or how they got there.

Larry jumped in his pickup and headed up the hill to the disgusting shed where he knew Roscoe hung out. Roscoe was not there. His cot was there, but no other belongings. When he got back to the house he discovered that the $500 that Larry normally kept in the cookie jar was also gone. Larry fumed.

His first inclination was to call the police, but he was not sure whether there had been any legal infractions. Probably more to the point he didn't want the cops sniffing around his wheat ranch. He owned this piece of the world, and it was his to do as he pleased. It would have gratified him no end to get Ross out of his hair, but not be worth it if the trade off was having a bunch of gov'ment men swarming around.

Then, incongruously, he thought about the visit that Grace and Jenny had paid him a couple months back. If he called, he would prefer to talk to the younger one. She had been forthcoming with the exact reason they were looking for Ross. Larry remembered the older one as being evasive, or at least not fully disclosing. When he looked at the card that had been given to him he saw it was Grace's, who he remembered was the older of the two. He decided not to make the call. Anyway, all they had wanted was to find out whether Ross was alive or not.

࿐

Roscoe got to Canada, on the last day of March. As soon as he was settled into the Vancouver Backpacker House he sent Margo a text message. "Mother dear. I'm all right. I'll be back to see you in a month or so."

Margo picked up the message and cried.

࿐

Over the next several days, Larry made a daily trip to Ross's new facility and observed an increasing number of fish accumulating in the settling pond, as well as in the interior tank. Ross had set his pump control timers so that the pumps operated only during the night, and as a consequence Larry observed no flow of water. He knew nothing about salmon anyway, except that when Margo cooked it for dinner he would leave the table and go to the refrigerator for salami and

180

Coors. It seemed apparent to Larry that the fish were swimming up the flume into the pond, but the mystery to him was that there was no water in the flume. It was an easy puzzle to solve, but he was too sore at what Ross had accomplished under his very nose to think straight. He had no patience to trace the path of the water through the pumping array. And did not even see that the electrical service panel was fitted with electronic timers.

Larry's only recourse was to rail at Margo, which he did. It was a common scene, and Margo had developed skill at bobbing and weaving in such a way that the verbal blows were parried and Larry never was quite sure if she knew what was on his mind.

A couple of weeks passed and the settling pond continued to fill incrementally day by day. On the second Thursday in April, Larry checked out the situation before leaving for his regular trip to Portland. It appeared to him that the number of fish had increased more than on any previous day.

The wheat ranchers gathered at the Odd Fellows Hall in Portland, and he mentioned his problem to some of them. The almost universal response was some variation of, "Hell, that's not a problem. Maybe you should give up wheat and become a fish monger. Hahaha." The one exception had been Rocky Sherbine, who found the situation both interesting and perplexing.

These sorts of replies did not please Larry at all, so he stopped talking about it. As he drove home after the meetings had ended, he realized that the list of people he was upset with consisted of several of his closest friends in the wheat business, his wife, Margo, and his stepson. The first two on the list were troublesome, but being angry at Ross was a constant. The happiest years of Larry's life were when Ross was away at college and working in the bug plant, as Larry called it.

The next morning when Larry checked the pond, it looked like a hatchery. Huge Chinook salmon were so thick that it appeared that you could walk across their backs and never get your feet wet. At that moment, he decided he needed to call somebody.

๛

Angie texted Deanna: "Hang onto your hat. The run is on."
Deanna texted back: "Still slow here."
On the next break, Angie texted again. "Sup?"
Deanna texted back: "Probably tomorrow."
The next night Deanna expected her counts to start registering the fish that Angie had counted at The Dalles, but the numbers were still low. When the same result continued on the following night Deanna became perplexed and called Jill West at the Bonneville counting station. She knew that Jill had reported high counts the last two nights, so Deanna sensed that there was something amiss. Jill confirmed that her counts had begun to increase rapidly on the order of what Angie had observed at The Dalles.

Deanna had been a counter long enough to know that there was little variation in the time it took the run to progress upstream, and for some reason there was a delay between The Dalles Dam and the John Day Dam. She had a number to call in an emergency which would awaken an FPOM biologist. The biologist, Frank Wills thanked her, wrote something on a note pad, and went back to sleep.

The next morning Frank made calls to a contact from each of the agencies represented on FPOM. The earliest they were all able to convene was Monday – two days hence.

๛

Henry Stagshin, an eighteen-year old high school student from the Yakama Nation, had built a birch bark canoe with his father as a special project for their Indian Crafts class at the reservation school. On Sunday, he put the canoe in the water at a dock near Biggs Junction, intending to paddle westward along the Oregon shoreline of the Columbia. As he passed the point of confluence with the Deschutes River, he saw salmon schooling on the left bank of the Columbia. It appeared that at the point of confluence, many Chinook were heading up the Deschutes. Many more were schooling in the eddies formed by the Deschutes inflow.

Henry was met by his father at their prearranged spot. On the trip back home to the Yakima reservation, Henry told his father that they should get their fishing equipment and return to the canoe. His father asked Henry why, and Henry said that they would catch salmon. Without requiring any further explanation Henry's father drove them back to the canoe, which they paddled to the site of the schooling Chinook. There, within a matter of a very few minutes, they caught ten large Chinook salmon. "We must tell no one," Kiyiwa Stagshin told his son.

"I will tell no one," replied his son.

On the following Monday the member agencies of FPOM met at the Bonneville Power Administration conference room. Subsequent counts at Bonneville Dam, The Dalles Dam, and John Day Dam confirmed the discrepancy that Deanna had reported to Frank Wills. The agencies that were present were NOAA Fisheries, the Columbia River Indian Tribe Fishery Council, the Corps of Engineers, the Bonneville Power Administration, and the Oregon, Washington, and Idaho Departments of Fish and Wildlife. None of the biologists present had a ready explanation for what might have caused the delay in migration from The Dalles Dam upstream to the John Day Dam. Suggestions included releasing more water at the upstream dams to increase the current; a helecopter fly-over with a combined dye release at John Day Dam to see if there was a deviation in the normal flow pattern; igniting small depth charges at intervals to enable fish counts at each explosion site; and divers to inspect subsurface conditions. Nobody thought to suggest a boat tour. The representative from the CRITFC was Kiyiwa Stagshin, who had not spoken during the meeting. "What do you think?" the NOAA fisheries guy asked."

"The plan appears to be suitable to the task." said Kiyiwa solemnly.

CHAPTER THIRTY-FIVE

A press release from the Corps of Engineers made page two of The Dalles Chronicle, and page six of the Sunday Oregonian. It read:

"An apparent discrepancy in Chinook salmon counts is puzzling agency representatives of FPOM, the Fish Passage Operations and Management Committee. 'Upstream migrant salmon are taking longer than usual to navigate the reach of river between The Dalles Dam and John Day Dam,' said Bill Reft, a spokesman for the Corps of Engineers. 'Efforts are underway to identify and remedy the problem,' he said. Reft added that representation on FPOM includes seven agencies. 'We have met and are implementing an action plan which we are confident will help the migrants along their way to their natal spawning riffles.'"

The news item got a thirty second early news slot on two of the local television networks. Although seen by Lem Russell and Rocky Sherbine, neither gave it much thought. But Larry Jepson also saw it, and he wondered right away if there was a connection between the migration delay and what was going on in the wild rice seed freezing building. Remembering that at the wheat ranchers meeting Rocky had shown some interest in his situation, he decided to call him. Rocky's dealings with Larry were few and far between, but they had always gotten along better than some of the other guys Larry dealt with.

"Did you see that report on the news about the fish counts?"

"Yeah. Yeah, I did, Larry."

"It's got me a little worried."

"What do you think is going on, Larry?"

"I don't know, but I have a feeling that what's happening at my place is somehow linked to that newscast. One thing I didn't tell you on Thursday is that Ross has up and disappeared again."

"What are you going to do?"

"I'm open to suggestion. That's why I called you, Rock."

"Well, if it was me, I'd get in touch with one of those women I sent down to see you. They were on the track of something to do with your stepson. My guess it that they'll either know something, or figure something out about it."

"They just thought he might have been murdered or something. I thought of calling them, but I don't see how what they wanted to know even fits in to what I've discovered."

"Larry, what they told me was that Ross was missing. Since you know he was hiding out at your place, it means that he was doing something that he didn't want anyone to find out about. Even if they can't help you figure out what he's done there, they'd want to know. You should give em a call, Larry."

"All right, I'll give them a call."

"Okay, Larry. Let me know if you find out anything."

CHAPTER THIRTY-SIX

On Monday Henry and Kiyiwa Stagshin caught ten more salmon from their birch bark canoe and returned to the reservation. They could have caught that many with their hands in the same amount of time, but they used light equipment and fished like white men. Back home they gave away six large fish to good friends, but when asked where they had fished, they only said, "Columbia River."

Are you planning to go again tomorrow?" Redfeather asked in his aging gravelly voice.

"No."

Later Redfeather told his wife, "They will go. I will follow."

The following day Kiyiwa said to Henry, "Let's go." They got into their truck and drove around for a couple of hours and returned to the res. Henry knew why they were doing it, and kept an eye on the side view mirror. Sure enough he caught an occasional glimpse of Old Redfeather's truck.

"OIT," Kiyiwa told Henry.

Henry laughed. "Old Indian trick tricks old Indian."

ॐ

Grace had scarcely settled into her desk chair when the phone rang. She had a full agenda, and considered not answering but did. "Hello?"

"This is Larry Jepson."

187

Grace waited for several seconds to see if Larry would add something more. When he didn't she said, "Hello, Larry, what's up?"

"Who have I got?"

"This is Grace Summers."

"Okay, Grace, you may remember me? You may remember I'm the stepfather of the boy who worked for you and disappeared."

"I remember that. Of course."

"Well, first of all, he hasn't been murdered. When you were here, I sensed that he might be around. There's a filthy shack on the BLM land that borders my property. The guy stays up there sometimes. But now I think he's disappeared again."

"Do you have any idea where he went?"

"No. But I think I told you that I had given him a free hand – and a free ride, as well – to develop wild rice production up here. He had me convinced that it was possible and would be profitable. I should have kept closer track, but that train has left the station. I discovered too late that whatever he's doing down there at the freezer building is causing salmon to come up through the effluent flume and right into the settling pond. A lot of them are even jumping into an interior tank. I was just wondering if you know anything about that."

"No. I can't imagine what's going on. I had heard that he was seen in The Dalles, so at least I knew he hadn't been murdered. What you're telling me does sound a little strange."

"It's not a little strange. It's very strange. It was on the news."

"What was on the news?"

"Well, they say that fish are being counted down at Bonneville and The Dalles, but they're not reaching the John Day Dam. At least they aren't ascending the ladder there. The news says the agencies have an action plan to fix the problem, but nobody's shown up here. My guess is that they don't know diddly squat, and they're just putting out fake news. That's the new fad, you know."

"Not so new, I expect."

"Well, anyhow, I need somebody who can figure out what's going on. I thought that might be you. Rocky thought the same thing."

"Have you called Lem Russell?"

"Nope."

"Why don't you call him?"

"The cops up here are just a bunch of guys who make sure that when you drive through town you don't go too fast. They don't know how to cope with a mystery. Not only that but I think Lem Russell still thinks that I killed Joe Toth."

"I still think that's your best way to proceed though. I wouldn't know what else to do."

"I wonder if I might talk to Jenny."

"She won't be able to shed much light on the situation, but I'll put her on."

Grace handed the phone to Jenny, who listened to an abbreviated account of what Larry had told Grace. Jenny started off by saying, "Did you say that the same day the salmon started showing up at your place was the day that Ross disappeared?"

"Pretty close. Probably the same."

"If I fly up to Portland would you be able to pick me up?"

"Just let me know, we can work something out. Do you have a separate phone number?"

Jenny gave Larry her number and got his. "You're not going up there Jenny. I need you here," Grace admonished.

"One, or both of us has to go. If you won't go, I'll fly up there myself. Listen, Grace, three or four days won't make or break your project. You are going to succeed, but right at this moment you wouldn't be able to tell me the exact day that you'll have the big breakthrough. It might be in two months, or it might be tomorrow. What I'm saying is that three or four days is not going to matter."

"I'll think about it."

"That means yes."

"No it doesn't. It means *no*."

"I think it should mean yes."

"All right, I can get by without you until Thursday. You go and I'll try to keep our venture going."

"Larry said he'd meet us at the airport in Portland."

"He'll meet you, not us. Be back by Thursday morning."

Jenny went online to see what the options were for flying from Oakland to Portland. There were several, and she made a reservation on Alaska Airlines for that afternoon. Then she called Larry and told him that she would arrive at 3:00 o'clock.

Ω

On the ride eastward along the Columbia, Larry told Jenny that Rocky and Terri Sherbine had invited her to stay with them. "The missus was a little skeptical," he said of his own wife. Terri has a room for you and wants you to fill her in on what you know, and what you think is going on."

"Have you walked down along the flume to where it goes into the river?"

"Nope. Now that's a good idea. I don't know why I didn't do that already. You've already earned the cost of your flight up here."

"I doubt that, but we might find something out."

"You ought to be a detective."

"I've been thinking the same thing, Larry."

Larry drove his truck to the level spot next to the building. Jenny could hardly believe what she saw when she looked at the pond. It was brim full of squirming leviathans. As some leaped the cascading flow from inside the building, others would slide back into the pond. It sounded and even looked

190

as if the entire pond was boiling. "How far is it to the end of the flume?" Jenny asked.

"'Bout a half mile. It's not too rugged. Want to take a look?"

"I sure do."

They picked their way along the wooden structure until they got to a small beach on the bank of the Deschutes. Although the aggregation of fish at the bottom of the flume did not look anything like what she had seen in the pond at the top, she could still see in the fading light that there was a concentration of salmon for a hundred-foot radius around the outfall. "They like your wild rice project, Larry," she said with a smile.

"Do you want to look inside the building?" he asked.

"Tomorrow. By the time we get back up the hill I'll be ready to give up for the day. I might bring Terri down if you don't mind."

"So you knew Roscoe when he was working at the bug plant?"

"No, Grace just told me about him. I'm trying to figure out why he has been so furtive during the past couple of months. It's really evident that he had a carefully scripted plan here. I can't wait to look inside the building, but as I said, I'm a little weary. Besides it's dark."

"There's lights in there."

"Tomorrow."

"Even though you didn't know him, I'll drive you by his hideout. One look at it will tell you something about the guy. I don't know what, but something."

Larry drove his truck slowly up the narrow rutted path to the old cabin. As soon as she opened the truck door to look at the cabin, Jenny could smell it. "That's the smell of death," she said.

"Just smells like shit to me."

"That, too. Another thing you're right about – this tells me something about Roscoe, but like you said, I don't know what it is." Without entering, they peered through the door. "I've seen enough," Jenny said.

Larry drove along a connector loop that took them back to the driveway. It was four or five miles up to the Sherbine place, and when they arrived Larry escorted Jenny up to the door.

CHAPTER THIRTY-SEVEN

Terri met Jenny at the door with a hug. "We're so glad you're here, Jenny. Ever since Rocky and I saw the news broadcast we have been aching to talk about it, but no one up here seems to care."

"I haven't seen the news. What did they say?"

Terri had discovered the news article on page six of the Oregonian and showed it to Jenny. "This is about the same as what they showed on the five o'clock news. They just showed a few shots of the dams and some fish swimming in the fishways, but the text was the same."

Jenny described what she had seen at the pond, the flume, and at the river. "I told Larry that I'd like to bring you along tomorrow to check out the so-called wild rice freezing facility, and he said that would be fine."

"Thank you, Jenny. That will be great. Hey, between us, maybe we can figure out what's going on. I shouldn't even say between us, because you seem to be a lot better at putting all these clues together than I am. You can be Nancy, and I'll be George."

"Sounds good to me. Too bad I don't know what it means."

"Oh my gosh. You're way too young to know who Nancy Drew is."

"I must be, because I don't know who she is."

"No worries, you just be Jenny and I'll be Terri."

Rocky emerged from somewhere and greeted Jenny. "What do you think is going on, Jenny?"

"I think we're going to find out tomorrow. Terri's going to go with me down to the building that Roscoe built."

"Maybe you'll see the maiden all forlorn."

"What's that supposed to mean?"

"Oh, I don't know, Jenny. Just part of an old rhyme."

"What's it rhyme with?"

"Oh, gosh, Jenny, as I remember, she milked a cow with a crumpled horn."

"If this was a Poirot mystery, that information would fit in somehow."

"Well, Jenny, you never know, do you. Anyway, keep me posted."

ᛒ

The next morning they called Larry to let him know that they were on the way. Terri moved some stuff out of the way so Jenny could get into the cab of the truck and they headed down the hill.

Larry met them at the building, and they all went in together. There were a couple dozen salmon flopping around on the floor around the tank and several that had died. The pumps were not running, so no salmon were entering the building, but it was clear to Jenny that if Larry was telling the truth and this was Roscoe's doing, that he had convinced the upstream migrants that this was where they were supposed to spawn. "Roscoe has scented the water, somehow," she said. "He imprinted them and then he brought them back here with the same scent that he used to imprint them."

It only took a minute or two to find a reservoir with a drip line running into the two thousand gallon tank. "I wonder what he used. Too bad Grace's lab isn't here. She could analyze the composition of whatever it is that's dripping water into the tank."

"What would it be?" Larry asked.

"It could be anything. Anything that had some particular smell that would dominate any natural odors that were in the water where these fish originally came from. My guess is that they came from a hatchery. It would be easy to imprint them all in a place where they were concentrated into one small area, like in a hatchery."

Terri said, "I can't believe this. What were you doing when they were building it, Larry?"

Larry squirmed imperceptibly. "Ross was so enthusiastic that I let him have a free hand. When I'd ask him questions, he would tell me to leave him alone – that he was going to make us rich. Ross never finished anything he started, so I thought I'd let him do this project where I could give him a push if he gave up on it. I never needed to do that. I've never seen the boy so organized. But as I've said, a lot of what he was doing, he was pretty secretive about."

Jenny seemed surprised. "Yet he was living in that dump you showed me. How did he manage such a huge project from up there?"

"I don't know, but he did it."

"And you financed all of this?" Terri said, still incredulous at what she was looking at.

"He had sales figures that looked pretty good to me. He convinced me that we were going to make some good money out of wild rice."

"I think we need to let somebody know where the salmon are going," Terri said.

"I'm in a heap of trouble, I suspect," Larry guessed. "Ross has disappeared. Nobody is going to believe that I let this get built without having anything to say about it."

"This is amazing. I first got involved with this because Grace needed to find Roscoe. Now we need to find him again."

"I'm not sure that'll do any good. He'll just say he didn't have anything to do with it." Larry offered.

"Won't the contractors support your story, Larry? You told Rocky that they changed the design several times during the construction. Roscoe must have been telling them what to do."

"Well, even if it means I'm in trouble we have to tell somebody about this."

Jenny then said, "I wonder what would happen if we turn on the pumps and stop the drip. It's obvious that this drip system is what's attracting the fish. If you start running well water past them maybe they'll go back down to the Columbia River and continue swimming upstream."

"Well, it can't do any harm, I guess," Larry said, with a glimmer of hope in his voice.

He went to the panel to turn on the pump and discovered the timers that had been installed to control the flow and apparently the drip mechanism. The reservoir containing the scented water was still half full, but if they turned off the drip, they could dispose of the scented water later. Larry disengaged the timers and turned on the pump. Most of the salmon faced into the flow, but none of the three could discern any net movement in either direction.

"Let's give it some time," Jenny said.

"I don't know how we're going to pass the time without watching these fish," Larry said.

"W'ell go up to our place and have an early lunch," Terri said.

"That's a kind offer, Terri. I don't think Margo would be good company right now. She's more nervous than a long tailed cat in a room full of rocking chairs."

Within minutes of arriving, Terri had set out an array of food that looked like a breakfast buffet at the Ritz. They all filled plates and attempted conversation, but it was clear that what was on everybody's mind was what to do next.

Jenny said, "One mystery is what will these imprinted salmon do if they can't find the scent that they imprinted on?"

"We don't even know if they'll leave my place. Let's go back down there and see if they're leaving."

"This food is doing me a lot of good," Jenny said. "We could eat a few more bites and then go back down."

Terri agreed, and they ate with little conversation for a half hour or so before returning to the freezer building.

When they opened the door they were surprised to see that the two-thousand gallon tank only had a few salmon left in it. The pond that the tank spilled into was still roiling with salmon, but everyone thought that there appeared to be fewer of them than before.

Jenny said, "Let's take a couple gallons of this stuff down to the river and dump it in at the bottom of the flume."

"That might not be such a good idea," Terri said. "It might block the ones that were swimming up. It would also guide them up the Deschutes. We need them to stay in the Columbia. Maybe we should try to put some into the hatchery outfalls."

"You're right, Terri, but now that you say that I'm thinking we should just leave the scent drip off and see what happens. It already looks like the fish are leaving."

Terri then said, "We could go down to the bottom of the flume and see if it looks like more fish are leaving than entering."

"Great plan," Jenny said enthusiastically.

"They carefully walked down the hill alongside the flume and when they got to the bottom, it was evident that no fish were entering. As they watched, they saw a number of salmon falling backward out of the flume and back into the river. There were also fewer salmon visible in the eddies at the mouth of the Deschutes. "This is great news," Larry said. "Maybe we don't even need to tell anybody. I'll get the contractors out here tomorrow to tear this thing apart and nobody will be any the wiser."

"I'll keep the secret," Jenny said.

"So will I," said Terri.

They slowly ascended the hill back to the rice freezing facility. At the top, it appeared that there were fewer salmon in the settling pond. "Lookin' good," Jenny said.

CHAPTER THIRTY-EIGHT

Rocky and Terri were meeting friends in The Dalles that night so they gave the Jenny the choice of joining them or staying at their house. She asked if they'd drop her off at the movie theater. They did that and arranged a meeting place after. Jenny treated to an ice cream cone after which they returned to the Sherbine ranch house and turned in.

Jenny and Terri had talked with such enthusiasm about what they had found the previous day that Rocky wanted to go down to the Jepson place and check it out. They met Larry at the building the next morning, and although the settling pond was still roiled, there were no fish visible.

"I think they're gone," Rocky said.

"Glory to God," Larry said.

"Awesome," Jenny said.

Terri smiled.

Rocky then asked, "What are you going to do now, Larry?"

"I'm going to get the construction crew out here as quick as I can and tear this god damn flume out. That's the first thing. Then I'll figure out what I can do with this building and modify it. It's got to be good for something. I'll tell you one thing – if Roscoe's smart he won't show up around here anytime soon. Anytime at all, I should say."

"The news report might be interesting tonight," Rocky said.

Jenny wondered out loud, "That's if they continue upstream. They might be so confused that they won't know where to go. You know, I rode part way out here from the east with a guy who knew a lot about salmon. He's the guy who first told me about their uncanny ability to find their way back to where they were hatched. Anyway, I wonder if they have a sense of smell like a dog. You probably know this but I've heard that a dog breaks one smell into a whole bunch of different components just like my father did with every aspect of life. If salmon can do that – separate the different parts of a smell, I mean – they could still find their way to their natal area by sniffing out the other components. That's what we should hope for anyway."

„

That night they all watched the news. Rocky, Terri, and Jenny watched at the Sherbine house and Larry watched it at his place with Margo, who couldn't understand his interest, since he usually complained if the TV set was even on at all. He didn't tell her anything. "Just interested in what's gong on," he said.

No such inquiry at the Sherbine residence. All were rapt as the Asian woman at KPTV in her most upbeat intonations, told them,

> *"Where have all those salmon been? Well, since last night they've been swimming up the fishway at John Day Dam. But nobody is saying why it took them so long to get there. 'That seems to be anybody's guess,' said Frank Wills, a biologist from the fish passage operation and management program. Wills told us that the FPOM three point action plan had yielded the results they had hoped for. 'Moreover,' said Wills, 'we never had any doubts about the run itself. Aberrations are the norm rather than the exception.' Finally, apparently waxing jocular, he added, 'You know the old saying, where there's a Wills there's a fishway.'"*

"I wonder what the three-point action plan was." Jenny asked.

Rocky said, "One, get you up here, Jenny; two, have you interpret why the salmon were swimming up the flume; and three, figure out how to reverse it so they'd go back to the river."

"No one will ever know," she said.

ॐ

Larry called his contractor the next day and told him to remove the wooden flume. "The sooner the better," he said.

"We can get to it tomorrow, Larry."

CHAPTER THIRTY-NINE

Christopher Debose was a life-long resident of Dufur. Now sixty-eight years old, he was contemplating the sale of his contractor business, one of the biggest in the Hood River Valley. He already thought he'd worked too long. He had more money than he could ever spend, and he was one of the best sailboarders in the gorge. The local boarders all knew him, but when an outsider would see him it was always, "Look at that old man," or something similar.

His feelings about Larry Jepson were mixed. More accurately, he considered Larry a friend and also a source of a lot of work over the years. The last job had put a bundle of money in his pocket, but it came at the expense of his foreman and often himself having to deal with the kid, Ross, who did not seem to be able to communicate what he was trying to accomplish. Over the course of the construction, there was one change order after another, and they all came at the eleventh hour. Moreover, there was always some kind of secrecy involved. "Keep this quiet," or "This is just between you and me." Chris did not achieve the success he had by being naive. He knew that the kid was up to something dishonest, but he couldn't figure out what it might be. He didn't have much knowledge about rice culture, so he was not able to judge whether the story he'd been given about wild rice was realistic. He thought it could be, but he also was certain that anybody who dealt with him in the sneaky way the kid had was probably dealing him a ration of bullshit.

When Larry called and told him that he wanted the flume torn out Chris was somehow not surprised. He felt as if all his doubts and suspicions had been confirmed. Larry had told him it was urgent. Pretty damn strange, he thought, but Larry was paying extra for Chris to rearrange his schedule, so he was not going to complain. He knew that Larry had finally realized that the kid had done something that needed to be undone.

Chris decided to oversee the job himself rather than send his foreman, who already was at his wit's end. Chris showed up bright and early with a crew of eight to commence the de-construction. The workmanship had been excellent consisting of heavy lumber fastened with lag screws, the latter actually making the deconstruction less difficult than 40d nails would have been. They began at the top of the flume where it came out of the settling pond dam, and worked downward toward the river.

At 11:42, Muñeco, one of the laborers, made a discovery that caused him cross himself and then yell to the guy closest at hand, who happened to be Teodoseo Raygoza. "*Hey, Teo, mira lo que he encontrado. Apurate, Cuate.*"

"We better let the boss take a look," Teo told him. They put down their tools and walked up the hill to where Chris was talking to Jenny and Terri, who had arrived an hour or so after the deconstruction had begun. Although Muñeco had made the discovery, Teodoseo's English was better, so it was he who said, "Can I talk to you a minute?"

"Sure. What's up?"

"Maybe you better come down here, boss."

"Excuse me, Ladies," Chris said, "sounds like something important." He accompanied the two laborers down the hill.

Although a thin layer of soil covered it, the skeleton was otherwise as clean as if were hanging in a biology laboratory. The flesh and connective tissue were gone, but the bones themselves were in their proper places with respect to each other. They were not bleached as if they had been exposed to the sun, but were beige in color. "Jesus H. Christ," Chris exclaimed.

"No way," said Muñeco.

Chris stood looking at the discovery for a full minute before he spoke. Finally he said to his two laborers, "Take a break. Go have your lunch."

"Okay, Boss. What you gonna do?" Teodoseo asked.

"I don't know yet."

The laborers climbed back up the hill while Chris stood gaping at the skeleton, considering his next move. He liked and trusted Larry, but he'd been jerked around so much on this project that even before the grisly discovery he was up to his eyeballs with suspicion. He took out his cell phone and after a quick search of the number, called Lem Russell. "Lem," he said, "I think you'd better come out to the Jepson place."

"I'm about to have lunch with the mayor," Lem said.

"We just found a skeleton out here. Human."

"Oh. That's different. I'll come on over then. Maybe it's Joe Toth."

"Should I tell Larry?"

"Sure. When you tell him try to notice if he's surprised or not. I'll be right over."

When Chris got to the top of the flume Larry was there talking to Jenny and Terri. "Larry," Chris said, "we just uncovered a skeleton down there."

"What kind?"

'Human."

"Damn," was all Larry said. Chris couldn't tell whether he looked surprised or not.

"Does that surprise you?" Chris asked.

Larry looked at Chris like Chris was out of his gourd. "What the fuck kind of a question is that?"

Chris realized the stupidity of the question and apologized.

"It's got to be Joe Toth," Jenny said.

"My god, how would you come up with that?" Terri asked.

"Well, we know he's been missing. They suspected murder, but it's hard to prove someone's been murdered when there's no *corpus delicti*."

"What's that mean, anyway?" Terri asked.

"I don't know. It's just what they always say on TV."

Chris said, "Well, Lem Russell is on his way over. He's the local police sergeant. When I called him, he also mentioned Joe Toth. Great minds think alike, I guess."

"Well, it makes sense that it's Joe Toth," Jenny said. "He was married to Margo Jepson, and here we are at the Jepson ranch. Too many coincidences for it not to be Joe. It will be easy to check out who it is by looking at the teeth. That's another thing I know from TV. Plus, I've been reading some criminology. I wonder if Lem has ever investigated a skeleton finding before. I doubt there are many in Dufur."

"Well, he'll know about the teeth deal," Terri said. "Everybody knows that."

"That just tells you who it is," Jenny said. "He has to try to figure out how he died and all that. It might be hard to do unless they find a bullet hole in his head. I'm familiar with that because my own father put one in his. Which brings to mind that even if there's a bullet hole, it doesn't prove the guy was murdered. I mean he could have committed suicide."

Chris had not spoken since his ill-advised question about whether Larry was surprised, but finally said, "That skeleton was not there when we built the flume. We would have seen it. There was only an inch or so of soil over the top of it, so my guess is that somebody placed it there after the flume was already built."

Jenny looked at Larry. "You're going to be a suspect. You probably already thought of that."

"It crossed my mind, but even though I was never too fond of Joe, I never would've killed him. I don't kill people."

"By the way," Larry turned to Chris, "how big is that skeleton down there? Joe was pretty small, so wouldn't he have a small skeleton."

"I don't know. I didn't even notice. When you find a human skeleton it's such a shock that maybe you don't notice the size. I didn't anyway."

"It's gotta be Joe Toth, for sure," Jenny said.

CHAPTER FORTY

Lem arrived at about 1:30. "You must have decided to have lunch with the mayor after all," Chris commented.

"Nah. But I did have to eat something after all. Couldn't come over on an empty stomach. I went over to Freddie Meyers and got one a them cooked chickens. Lord, I wonder what they do to them things to make em so dang tasty. I figure they soak em in something. Anyway, that's what I had – chicken and chicken. There's a couple bites left in the truck if any of you want to partake."

After a round of no-thank-yous, Lem said, "Well, shall we go take a look?" Then, to Chris, "You can send these guys home; all maybe but the guy who found the skeleton. This could take awhile. I don't think you'll want to pay these guys for standing around while we figure things out."

Chris sent all but Muñeco home. Muñeco crossed himself again, and said, *"Bueno."*

They all traipsed carefully down the hill to the skeleton site. The looked like a bunch of scouts trying to qualify for a hiking merit badge. Jenny and Terri walked together. "I wonder what he'll do," Terri commented.

"Wouldn't it be awesome if he took out a big magnifying glass and started inspecting the bones?" Jenny said.

"Well, I know that Sherlock Holmes did that, and he's famous, so it must be a good technique."

When they arrived at the skeleton, Lem asked everyone to stand back while he checked around. I see at least ten different boot prints here. Probably none belonging to the perp."

Lem had a camera and took a few pictures. Then he said to Muñeco, "Is this how you found it?"

"*Si señor. Exactamente,*" Muñeco crossed himself again.

"You didn't touch the bones?"

"*No, no. Tenia miedo.*"

"What does that mean?"

"It means he was scared," Terri said.

"Somebody put these bones on this piece of plywood and used it for a stretcher. Obviously this guy didn't die here."
Lem walked back to the skeleton and knelt down beside the skull. He removed a magnifying glass from his jacket and inspected the skull. "Looks like a pretty good crack right over his left eye socket here," he mumbled.

"How cool is that?" Jenny uttered.

Terri whispered, "It worked for Sherlock; I guess it works for Lem."

Jenny blurted out, "That's the skeleton of Joe Toth."

"How do you know?" Lem asked her.

"Logic."

"We usually like to list all the evidence that leads to any given conclusion," Lem said, suddenly sounding more like a police sergeant than a hay seed.

"You should measure the skeleton," Jenny suggested.

"You can check dental records, too, right?" Terri asked.

"We sure could do that, Mrs. Sherbine. One thing though."

"What's that?"

"That doesn't work too good unless the guy has had dental records. This guy doesn't have any fillings. Maybe he never went to the dentist."

"Oh, that."

"Well, I think Jenny here might have hit the nail squarely on the head about who this guy is"

"How can you be so sure?" Larry asked.

"I can't. Just a hunch. I'm going to have to get this guy down town. It was nice of whoever put him here to put this here board under him. The problem I see is that I can't get my truck down here. That makes it something of a mystery how someone got him down here."

"Maybe it was two people," Jenny offered. "Maybe they carried the board down here like it was a stretcher."

"That's how we're going to get him up to the truck. Pretty good thinking, Jenny."

Jenny then added, "You keep calling it him. It could be a woman. It's a pretty small skeleton."

"The reason I'm calling it *him* is that Giuseppe was a man."

"I mean if it's not Joe Toth."

Lem ignored the comment, and asked Larry, Chris, Rocky, and Muñeco to carry the board up the hill. Muñeco mumbled something that sounded like *Chinga tu madre,* but did as he was told.

When they got to the top of the hill, Lem put the board in the back of his truck, and noted that there were actually two boards. One was badly rotted but the bottom one was old and weathered but not rotted. "Hasn't been there long," he said.

"I already told you that," Chris said.

"Well, Chris, when someone tells me something, I say to myself, 'That's either true, or it ain't true,'" Lem said. "If it turns out to be true it's more likely that the person who told me is not trying to hide something than if he tells me something that ain't true. The problem is, I can't always tell. So that board tells me more than just that it wasn't there very long. It tells me that what you told me wasn't a lie."

Jenny turned to Terri, "I bet this guy has never had a murder case in his life. But he's really getting down to the bare bones of the matter."

"You could be right. I don't remember any skulduggery like this before. Not around here. But don't forget that he used a magnifying glass. That shows some real savvy about murder investigation."

"Oh yeah. I forgot."

Before he got into his truck, Lem told Larry to follow him down to the police station in The Dalles. "I just have a few questions I need to ask you," he said, then added, "Give me a half hour or so. I've got to get this guy over to the morgue and fill out a few papers. I'll see you at the station in a half hour."

Rocky, who hadn't said much since Lem arrived, turned and said more to Larry than Lem, "Yeah, that's ol' Giuseppe all right. Not much doubt about that."

Lem overheard the comment and asked,"What makes you so sure?"

"Well, Lem, take a look at his leg bones, how they're bowed. Ol' Giuseppe was bow-legged. I don't know why. I don't think the guy ever got on a horse in his life. But he sure was bow-legged. I always thought the poor guy would have been an inch taller if he hadn't been so god damn bow-legged."

Terri looked at Jenny. "God, Jenny, my husband is a detective and I didn't even know it."

CHAPTER FORTY-ONE

After Lem drove off, Larry looked around and said, "I wonder why he wants to question me?"

As if not to hear Larry's comment, Chris said, "I'm going to head on back to my office. I'll make sure the guys are ready to come back and deconstruct the rest of the flume tomorrow."

Rocky then addressed Larry's concern. "I expect it's because the skeleton was found on your land, Larry. If you don't know anything about how it got there, you should be all right."

"I sure as hell hope so. I sure do."

∞

Lem cordially greeted Larry at the station. "Let's walk back here to the conference room," he said. When they got there, Lem appeared to change into a different man, "What the fuck is going on here Larry? You didn't kill that man so you could marry his wife did you?"

Larry was flabbergasted. All he could say was, "What?"

"What I said was, that's Joe Toth we found on your property, and I want to know why. I want to know why you killed him."

"I didn't kill him. I don't know where he came from. But I know that I had nothing to do with it." Larry could feel himself boiling over.

"How do I know that? You sure had a motive."

"Oh, bullshit. Go do some detective work, Lem. You can't just say I did it because it was on my land and because I married his wife. I never married her until five or six years after the guy disappeared. I sure as hell didn't know I'd ever marry her at the time he went missing."

"Larry, I think you were having an affair with Margo, and figured if you could get Joe out of the way that you could eventually marry her. You had to wait a few years, but you knew he wouldn't show up because you knew he was dead. You knew he was dead because you killed him."

Blood rushed into Larry's face and tears formed in his eyes. His hands unconsciously formed fists. Larry was a burly man who had once defended himself successfully against two bikers who, like Larry, thought he had murdered Joe Toth. One of the bikers wound up in the hospital and the other took off like a rabbit fleeing from a fox. Now, it took every bit of his will power to keep from unloading on the police sergeant with his enormous fist. Finally, he repeated his earlier comment. "Bullshit."

Lem did another complete about face. "Thanks for coming in, Larry. Where's Ross, by the way?"

The change of approach took Larry completely by surprise. "I don't know," he said. "He was around, but disappeared. I can't say exactly which day, but I went looking for him four or five days ago, and he was gone."

Almost as if he were talking to himself, Lem said, "That's probably about as long as Joe Toth has been under the flume. And speaking of that, what is that flume for anyway?"

"I'm embarrassed to say that I don't know. Ross built it as part of the project I let him do out at my place. He told me it was part of a grand plan of his to grow wild rice. The next thing I know it looked like the whole salmon run was coming into the building. Luckily, that Jenny-girl figured out why, and we sent em back to the river."

"I saw on the news that they had disappeared. They didn't mention anything about the flume though."

"I'm pretty sure they didn't figure it out."

"Are you telling me that something that Ross did caused the salmon to swim up the flume?"

"Yes I am, Mr. Russell. I don't understand how he did it or what he had in mind – especially since he disappeared when the salmon came up the flume."

"Larry, I wonder if you'd be willing to participate in a ruse with me?"

"I don't know, Sergeant. I'm not too sure what a ruse is. What did you have in mind?"

"I'd like to talk to Ross. If he thinks you've been arrested, he might come out of hiding and I'd be able to talk to him."

What makes you think he'd come out of hiding. He likes me about as much as I like him, which is none."

"I keep wondering what he was up to. He went to a lot of trouble to create a stir with that salmon heist. Whatever that was for, he's somewhere watching it with furtive pleasure. The other thing, Larry, is that both you and Chris Debose told me that there was no skeleton there when that flume was built. That skeleton has been lying around for twelve years getting cleaned by critters unknown. Then it shows up there. I'm pretty sure you didn't put it there, Larry, but I had to make certain. When I saw that you were about to punch me, I was convinced. I know I couldn't last one round with you."

"What's the ruse? How are you going to make Ross think I'm arrested?"

"With your permission, I'd like to call Margo and tell her. I'm pretty sure that the first thing she'll do is get in touch with Ross. I'm not sure what she'll say to him, but dollars to donuts Ross will head on back to the ranch. I just have this hunch that right this minute, Ross knows more than we do about what's going on. Not just with the salmon, but probably even with his old man's skeleton. Do you think the others will have told her about finding Giuseppe's skeleton?"

"I kind of doubt it, Sergeant. By the time I left to come down here, they had all left my place. You go ahead with your ruse if you want to. When Ross stayed out at my place he hid out in this old prospector's shack. I could go there and no one would see me."

"Ha, no one but Roscoe. That's the first place he'll go."

"Good point."

"You'll have to stay out at my place, Larry. It ain't the Astoria Waldorf, but it's home to me. Meanwhile you have to learn to call me Lem. You never were a suspect, in my mind, at least, but like I said, I just had to make sure."

"If you don't mind, I'd like to listen in on your phone call, Lem."

"Okay, Larry, here goes nothin. What's her number?"

Lem made a few notes on a yellow lined pad and then rolled the pencil back and forth in his fingers a few times. He picked up the receiver of his desk phone and then put it back and wrote something else on the pad. Finally he dialed the number.

"Hello?"

"Mrs. Jepson?"

"Yes, who's calling?"

"This is Sergeant Russell, ma'am. I'm calling from The Dalles police station. I'm afraid I have some disturbing news."

"Oh, dear, has something happened to Roscoe?"

"No, ma'am. It's not about Roscoe. Earlier today, we found the remains of your ex-husband's body. I'm not at liberty to give you any details, but I have arrested your present husband, Larry Jepson, in connection with Giuseppe's murder. He is being held without bail."

"Oh my dear. Can I talk to him, or come down and see him?"

"No ma'am. He is in custody here with no visitors. We may transfer him to the prison in Portland. I don't know what their visitation policy is over there."

"Oh my god. What will I do?"

"I'm sorry, Mrs. Jepson. I know this comes as a shock. We want to protect your privacy, so I don't intend to issue any statement to the press as yet. Again, I'm sorry to be the bearer of this unfortunate news."

Margo put down her phone and, looking out the kitchen window, ran her fingers through her hair. She then walked to the bathroom and looked into the mirror. Her face was flushed with irregular blotches. She washed her hands in the sink and dried them with a towel with *hers* embroidered on it. Then she returned to where she had left her phone and sent the following text to Roscoe.

"Larry has been arrested for the murder of your father."

Within a minute, a text came back.

"I'm leaving now for home. I will come to the house. It will take me thirteen hours. Please make sure no one is there."

CHAPTER FORTY-TWO

It took Jenny an hour to drink the Coors that Rocky gave her. When he offered another she accepted. The conversation at the Sherbines' was centered on the events of the day, which they all agreed were outside their usual realm. As usual Terri came up with a gourmet offering of delicious food – this time mostly Mexican. They discussed the curious placement of the skeleton as well as how the salmon attractant factored in, but up until then, they had not speculated about who had masterminded the whole thing.

Jenny opened that subject by saying, "I can't believe that Lem made Larry to go out to the station with him. There's no way that Larry did any of that stuff himself."

"I don't know, Jenny, do you think Lem wanted to interrogate Larry?" Rocky asked. "Maybe it was just to get some background on what's been going on out there."

"I sure hope that's it, because there's no way that Larry did that."

Terri offered, "I think Rocky's on the right track. Maybe Lem didn't want to question Larry as a suspect. He probably just wanted to get filled in on some of the history of the construction project and all that. One thing I know about Lem is that he's smart. He talks about that Freddie Meyer chicken like it's a big mystery, but that guy could cook one in his own home that tasted just like it."

Jenny then said, "You get what happened with the salmon, right?"

"Well yeah, I think so," Terri said. "But I don't see how the salmon and the bones are connected. That's why I'm saying that Lem probably just wanted to get as much information as he could from Larry."

"The part I know is this," Jenny said. "Those salmon were imprinted as they were smolting. That's the word they use to describe the yearlings that are getting ready for their downstream migration to the ocean. It's when they get this incredible memory of what their spawning riffle smells like. What I'm saying is for that drip set-up to work, it had to contain some scent that the smolts had already imprinted on. That means that someone put some foreign scent into the water when they were smolting. I don't know what you guys think, but my money's on Roscoe, one hundred percent. And the best bet for where he did it is in one or two of the hatcheries. Trouble is, of course, that is water over the dam, at this point – literally."

"I wonder if Larry's home yet," Rocky said. "I'll call his cell and find out what's going on." Rocky dialed Larry's number and got his voicemail. "That's peculiar."

"I could call Margo," Terri offered.

"I think the guy to call is Lem. I could do it, but maybe one of you guys should. I mean, you're the locals here. I just blew in from New York."

"You know a lot about salmon for an easterner."

"The main thing is that I have a better than average memory. So the first ride I got hitchhiking out here this truck driver picked me up and told me a whole bunch of stuff about salmon. Mike was the guy's name. When he was a kid he'd go out on a commercial fishing boat with his dad – out of Coos Bay, I think he said. Apparently his dad would teach him about salmon. It was pretty fascinating. Anyway, I think one of you guys should call Lem, but I will if you want. Lem kind of likes me, I think."

"You think he likes you?"

"Yeah. You know, he's pretty much got his eyes on me most of the time. There's no doubt at all that he'd like a little private time with me, but he's a gentleman and knows that the thought is all he's ever going to get."

Terri looked at Jenny like she was an alien. "I think you ought to call him, Jenny."

Jenny found his number on her phone and dialed.

"Lem Russell."

"Hi Lem, this is Jenny from this afternoon."

"What's up, Jenny?"

"Actually I called to ask you that same question. Have you figured anything out about our investigation?"

"After interrogating Larry, I had to arrest him for the murder of Giuseppe Toth. The investigation will continue, but that's all I can say for now. Where are you, Jenny?"

"I'm out at the Sherbines' place."

"Well, go ahead and let them know, but don't tell anyone else. We're still tying up some loose ends, but we don't want this to let this get around until a couple test results come in. So keep it under you hat for now."

"We'll do that, for sure, Lem – especially since you got the wrong guy." Jenny hung up in disgust. She then filled in the Sherbines on what Lem had said. They were equally chagrined.

The room now was filled with sympathy and anger paired with disbelief that it could even have happened. Rocky summarized their feeling when he said, "That's not Larry. I think Lem made a mistake this time."

CHAPTER FORTY-THREE

Roscoe arrived at the ranch house at about seven in the morning and his mother was waiting. They embraced, and Margo told Roscoe as much as she knew. She started with the Sergeant's call and then retraced what she had seen from the window. She saw the flume being torn down, and then she saw all the people gather in one place. Then the Sergeant showed up. It looked like they found something that had been stashed under the flume, and then they carried whatever it was up the hill on a board. It looked like a skeleton to Margo, but she could not be sure.

After she got the call from Sergeant Russell, she was pretty sure that what she saw was the skeleton of her former husband.

"Did they put him jail, Mother?"

"Yes, Ross, for murder. He'll never get out."

"Mother, now we can do whatever we want around here. I would have to consider this a nice turn in our lives."

"Oh, Roscoe, I don't know what I'd do without you. But you don't seem to understand that Larry is my husband."

"Well, I've done everything you ever asked me to. Without me you would have had to do them yourself. Have you visited Larry?"

"No, they won't let me."

"Mother, I don't know whether I should lay low for awhile, or whether I can be out in the open about being in town."

"For starters, I'd lay low."

"I was afraid you'd say that, but you're probably right."

∞

After eating breakfast at the Sherbines' Jenny asked Rocky if he'd ever seen the little cabin that Roscoe hid out in.

"No, Jenny. Can't say as I have."

"Larry took me up there, and for sure, it factors into this case somehow. It's filthy. Totally disgusting. I don't see how anyone could even go inside, much less sleep in there."

"Maybe we should go check it out, Jenny."

"I wonder if we need to tell Lem that we're going to go up there."

"I guess we should do that, Jenny. Yeah, I'd say that's probably a good idea."

Jenny already had Lem's number on her phone so she dialed it up.

"Sergeant Russell."

"Hi, Lem, it's Jenny."

"Hello, Jenny, How are things?"

"I was wondering if Rocky and I could go up and look around at Roscoe's hideout. And also if you'd like to go with us."

Lem thought for a second and then said, "Absolutely not. I can't tell you why right now, but you have to stay off the Jepson property and off the BLM land around it – all of it. It's a crime scene."

"Even up there? No one would even see us."

"Jenny, listen to what I say. Don't. That means *do not* go up there. Don't go onto the Jepson property at all and don't talk to Mrs. Jepson. Got it?"

"Yes, sir. I won't, that means *will not* go up there. I promise."

In his usual slow deep voice, Rocky said, "I guess we're not going up there, Jenny."

"I guess not. I would say we could sneak up, but Lem was adamant. He called it a crime scene, but he's not even up there. I believe Lem is up to something that he hasn't mentioned to us."

"Well, as Terri said, Lem is a smart guy. Sometimes he puts on a hay seed act, but I'd say the chances are good that he'll figure out this case. That is if you don't, Jenny."

The remark made Jenny feel like she belonged. But she knew that Grace wanted her back in the lab by tomorrow morning. "I wish I didn't have to go back, but I don't think Grace is going to let me stay up here."

"Do you want me to talk to her?"

"That would be awesome. What would you say?"

"I could say you're proving invaluable as a crime solver."

"Thanks, Rock, but I don't think Grace is going to buy into that."

"I guess we'll have to get you to the airport, Jenny."

"If you take me to the bus station in The Dalles, that should be good enough. Actually I probably have to leave in three hours. Luckily I didn't bring too much stuff – just a backpack."

"We can take you out to the airport in Portland. It's out on this end of town, so we won't even need to get into too much traffic. One thing I'd like to do before we leave is sit down with you and Terri and hear what you think might be going on. You're the one who had the ba... um, certainty to tell Lem he had the wrong guy. I'm just real curious to find out what you know, or at least what you think you know."

"Any time, Rocky. As you've probably noticed, I have a habit of blurting out things. It doesn't always mean I know what I'm talking about."

80

Terri fixed lunch and they sat on a sun porch eating sand-
witches. "Jenny's going to give us her theory of the crime,"
Rocky said.

"That makes it sound like I have one," Jenny said. I really
don't. But I can tell you what I think. One: Larry didn't do it.
That the skeleton was found on his property means nothing.
Anyone could have put it there. Two: Someone *did* put it
there. Three: The salmon theft, if you want to call it that, is
somehow part of the murder plot. Four: Lem doesn't think
Larry did it. He's got something up his sleeve. He's baiting a
hook. His insistence that we stay away from Roscoe's hideout may have something to do with his plan. That's all that
comes to mind. There really isn't anything new here, it's just
that I always like to break things down."

Terri said, "You're really amazing, Jenny. So you've got all
these things you think are true, but can you see how they re-
late to one another?"

"Not quite. Sometimes I think I see an answer, and then it
goes away, or I see that it's flawed. I wish I could hang with
you guys, but I gotta roll. I'm sorry."

"No worries. We'll let you know if there's anything new."

Jenny threw her backpack into Rocky's truck and got in the
back seat. Terri joined Rocky in front.

"Jenny," Terri said, "you have to come back up here and
explain what's going on. You're the only one that seems to
understand it."

"As I just told Rocky, I don't understand anything. I just try
to organize what we know."

As the truck was about to merge on to I-84 at Biggs Junction, Jenny's phone rang. It was Grace.

CHAPTER FORTY-FOUR

Not long into the phone call Jenny said to Terri, "Grace is coming up here. Tell Rocky he can turn around." The call lasted only a couple more minutes. Grace told Jenny that she was in a discussion that would bring some money and expertise into their company. She told Jenny that another company, the same one that had originally shown interest, had sent a merger proposal and Grace had sent back a counter proposal. All very complex, she said, but the end result was that while she waited for a response she thought it would do her good to get away from the lab for a few days.

"Yippee!" Jenny said when she shut off her phone. "Grace is on her way up. You know what that means? It means I don't have to go back."

"Jenny, that's wonderful," Terri said.

Rocky said, "Somehow I have a feeling that you and Lem are going to figure this thing out. Meanwhile, I guess we can make room for Grace at our place."

"Oh, sure, we can do that," Terri said.

"No. Grace already made reservations at the Balch. Plus she rented a car, so she can drive out to your place and we can bring her up to date on our crime solving mission."

౼

Lem Russell usually took his lunch to work in a brown bag, one of 500 such bags that he bought on the Amazon website. Today, he instead went home for lunch. There was some spaghetti left from last night's dinner, but he stopped at the grocery store for a loaf of rye bread. When he got to his home he found Larry reading his autographed copy of *Pampas Cat*. "How do you like that book?" he asked.

"One of the weirdest god damn things I've ever read. I don't read much because I'm always busy. I guess that's one good thing about being in jail is that you don't have to work twelve hours a day."

"Well, sorry to interrupt your reading, but I thought I'd bring you up to date on my investigation."

"Good. Hate to break away from this book, though. It's awesome."

"Well, Ross showed up at your place early this morning. He rode in on his little Honda trail bike, so he must have rode that thing all night long. When he got there, he went right up to the front door and was let in, no doubt by Margo. After about three hours, he went back to his Honda carrying a box – for now we'll guess it was full of groceries – and rode on his Honda back up the hill to his lair."

"How do you know that, Lem?"

"Oh, I had a hunch something like that might play out, so I sent a guy up to your place last night to watch. He parked in that little cherry orchard of yours so he wouldn't be seen. He told me he half froze to death waiting for something to happen, so imagine how cold Ross must have been riding that Honda of his all night from wherever he was."

"What made you think that might happen?"

"Oh, just a hunch, I guess."

"Lem, hunches don't just come out of nowhere."

"Well, Larry, was it you who built that building and the pond and the flume where we found the bones?"

"Nope. I'm sorry to say I paid the bills, but the real answer is no. I watched it go up, but I took Ross's word for it that it would be for growing wild rice."

"Okay, Larry, let's try a one-word answer this time. Did you design that whole complex?"

"No, I didn't."

"Okay, that's three, but it's the answer I expected. So who do you think did?"

"Well, Ross did. I told him he could."

"Okay, Ross builds this very unusual almost freakish compound and then disappears. Wouldn't you guess he'd come back? I mean he had some reason to build it. What do you think his reason was?"

"He sure got all those fish to come up there. I don't know how in the hell he did that, but he did. I have to confess that at some point I realized I didn't have the right terrain to grow rice. I don't know why it took me so long, but when Ross first presented this idea he was so convincing that I just decided to let him try it. If it was successful, it would have been a nice addition to what we're doing up there. If it failed, maybe he would disappear and I wouldn't have to put up with him any more. The building was almost finished by the time I put all of this together, so at that point I just got curious and decided to let him go through with whatever it was he was doing."

"What do you think he was doing?"

"That, I don't know. As you say, whatever it was, he decided not to be there when it happened."

ɞ

Grace arrived at the Sherbines' house and they took turns briefing her on the peculiar chain of events leading to the present moment. When it appeared that no one had anything to add, Jenny said, "Next stop, Lem Russell. Arresting Larry Jepson because a skeleton was found on his property does not make sense. If Lem is as smart as you have all said, it means he did it for some reason that he isn't going to talk about. We can start by asking to visit Larry. That poor guy is probably sweating bullets."

"You and Grace go," Rocky suggested. "You knew something was going on up here before any of us."

By the time Jenny and Grace got to The Dalles police station Lem had returned from his lunch with Larry. When the two women walked in he greeted them and invited them into the conference room. "What can I do for ya?"

"We're hoping to visit Larry."

"Can't"

"Why."

"No visitors allowed until we get a few questions answered."

"Lem, I can answer one for you. If we assume one question is 'did you arrest the right guy?' the answer is no. Larry is about as guilty as Grace, and you know it. You're playing games with someone, and I just hope it's not Larry. Larry is not only innocent, he's a nice guy."

"Don't stop believing in yourself, Jenny. Thanks for coming in, but maybe if you drop by tomorrow we can talk a little more. And remember, do not go onto the Jepson property. That's essential."

"Thanks," Grace said.

Jenny thought of saying nothing, but turned as the left and said, "You have my word." When they were underway to the hotel in Dufur, Jenny added, "Lem's gonna pull a rabbit out of his hat."

CHAPTER FORTY-FIVE

Back at their hotel, Jenny called Terri and told her about their visit with Lem. "Net zero," she said, "but I'm pretty sure that Lem is keeping a lid on some kind of plan he has in order to find out more."

"You keep saying that, but what do you mean?"

"I'm pretty sure that Lem thinks Roscoe killed his father. He knows that once Roscoe thinks Larry is out of the way, he'll return to the ranch. That's what I meant when I said he was baiting the hook. That's why Lem doesn't want anyone to go over there. At the moment, I can't figure out what he might plan to do when Roscoe comes back, but it's something. And I think that whatever it is will happen pretty quick, because he told me that he might be able to tell us a little more tomorrow, after some questions are answered. He also told me not to stop believing in myself after I scolded him for arresting Larry. So there's the case in a nutshell. My interpretation of that is that he was telling me that I'm right about Larry."

After Jenny hung up, Grace said, "Wow, Jenny, you got more out of that visit than I did. I thought the guy was just putting us off like a horse whipping his tail at a fly."

"As I've said before, I might be wrong. Just guessin'. By the way, Grace, you mentioned that the idea of a collaboration on your business is still alive. What's going on with that?"

"It's going on. We won't know any more than what I told you, until I hear back. The proposal was pretty aggressive. By that I mean it's very evident that they want a part of my action, so I feel pretty optimistic about getting whatever conditions I want into any agreement we might reach."

"That's really excellent if it's what you want. Even though I used to be your therapist, this appears to be a situation where I can't advise you, at least on the merit of the offer. But I can say this: if it's the right thing to do, your heart and your brain will be together. If one says yes and the other says no, proceed with caution, or not at all."

"Jenny, some of the guiding principles you come up with are the stuff of elders."

"I don't make em up. I hear em from elders – mainly my parents. They were platitudinal."

ဆ

Lem Russell called all four network television stations in Portland and left the following message at the news desk of each:

> "*The Dalles police report that the body of Giuseppe Toth, missing for over ten years, has been found on Larry Jepson's wheat ranch. Jepson's wife was previously married to Toth. Investigation into the cause of Toth's death is underway. No further information is available at this time.*"

Forty-five minutes later when the item was broadcast, Margo saw it and wondered if it meant that Larry had been cleared of suspicion. Would he be released, she wondered. Maybe he already had been and was on his way back to the ranch. Should she alert Roscoe to make sure that he wouldn't show up at the door? She had never even been up to the old abandoned cabin, and probably wouldn't have been able to walk to it even if she knew exactly where it was. It was already dark outside, and the terrain was difficult for a woman who never walked on a surface that was rougher than a sidewalk. As Margo considered the meaning of the new information, she became panicky. She knew where the path to Roscoe's hideout took off from their driveway, and the general direction he would go as he proceeded up the hill and wondered if she should sit in the window facing that direction and send a signal of some kind, perhaps SOS with a flashlight. She knew from movies that it was three shorts, three longs, three shorts. Maybe she should turn out all the lights and lock the doors. Either would be stupid, she knew. But knowing that didn't help her get over the panic. She went to her bedroom, got into bed and lay there for a couple of hours with her eyes open listening and watching for anything out of the ordinary. Nothing happened and finally she drifted off. When she awoke the next morning, all was normal, nothing amiss.

ଚ

Jenny and Grace had watched the same newscast in their hotel room. Jenny said, "It sounds like Lem finally wised up."

"Maybe we should go down to the station tomorrow and ask him what's going on."

"Good plan."

ଚ

Rocky and Terri also had seen the cast.

"I think we should give Jenny and Grace a call, don't you, Terri?"

"I'll call em right now." She touched out the number and after a brief chat, reported to Rocky that they, too, had seen the news and were baffled. "They're going to go down to talk to Lem tomorrow."

229

CHAPTER FORTY-SIX

Jenny and Grace entered the station the next morning. "We'd like to speak with Lem if possible," Jenny said.

"I'm sorry. He's in conference."

"Who with?" Jenny inquired.

"I'm sorry. That information is not something I'm at liberty to disclose," through pursed lips came the officious response.

"Well, whoopdeedo," Jenny said just loud enough to be heard. "How long will Lem be in conference?"

"I don't know."

"We're working with Lem on a crime," Jenny continued. "He might want to let us join him, whatever he's doing. He has called us twice in Berkeley to get our take on what's going on. Grace knows Roscoe Toth better than anyone. We're a reservoir of information in this matter. We're part of his team."

"I'd venture to guess you're wrong about that, ma'am."

At that moment the phone on the desk rang and the clerk answered. "Yes, Lem," she said.

"After a brief exchange, she punched in a two digit number and announced, "Lem wants you in the conference room, Warren."

"You should have told Lem that we were here," Jenny said in exasperation. Let's go, Grace. We appear to be out of the loop."

"You're right," Grace said. "I'm thinking that we should go talk to Margo Toth."

"Why?"

"We haven't talked to her. Something is going on. Maybe she knows what it is."

"There's something scary about that," Jenny said. "We've never seen her leave the house. Also, Lem told us to stay away from the Jepson property. He must have had a reason he didn't want us up there."

"Jenny, it's your call, but this may be an opportunity to learn something."

"Well, if you think so. We're sure not accomplishing anything here."

Grace suggested they pick up Terri on the way. Jenny agreed and they drove the Hyundai rental to the Sherbines' and picked her up. Terri suggested that they take Rocky along so they picked him up in his machine shop.

৪৩

Warren Brownell, the officer who had spent the night in the orchard and saw Roscoe arrive, entered the conference room. "Warren, I want you to go back up to the Jepson place. If Roscoe shows up, bring him in."

৪৩

At 10:30 Roscoe decided to disobey Margo's command and go down to the farmhouse. There were situations of utmost importance to discuss with her. There were things she needed to know in case she was ever questioned by the police. Besides that, he didn't even agree that hiding out was all that important right now. Larry was in the slammer and was the leading suspect in Giuseppe's murder. Things were unfolding just as he'd planned.

Feeling triumphant, he hopped onto his Honda and arrived at the farmhouse in less than fifteen minutes. Only minutes before his arrival, Jenny, Grace, Rocky, and Terri had been

231

invited in – somewhat reluctantly – by Margo. Taking in this unexpected scene, Roscoe's first words were, "What in the hell is Grace Summers doing here?"

"What are *you* doing here? I told you not to come down," Margo said.

As soon as Warren Brownell saw Roscoe arrive, he came down the hill from his surveillance point in the orchard. Everybody looked at each other without a word, until Jenny said, "Hey, what in the hell is going on here?"

"You tell me. I live here," Margo said.

Rocky then said, "Margo, a couple of days ago we found your ex-husband's remains, right down by your new construction site. At least we think it was your ex. Then Lem takes Larry with him back to town, like Larry's guilty of something. We're all anxious to find out what really happened, going all the way back to when Joe first disappeared."

Warren broke into the conversation by saying to Roscoe, "Lem Russell wants to see you down at the station Roscoe."

"Why? I didn't do anything."

"He wants to talk to you about something. He didn't tell me what."

"Screw that, I don't have to go. I need to talk to Mother."

"You are wrong about not having to go." Warren put a large hand on Roscoe's shoulder and pushed him hard enough so that Roscoe nearly fell. It was clear to everyone in the room including Roscoe, that Warren was in control. "Sorry to remove one of the guests from the party," Warren said as they exited.

Rocky then said, "What in the hell is going on here? First Larry and then Roscoe."

Margo followed with, "That's what I should be asking. What *is* going on?"

Jenny was next. "Margo, we have not met, but I am helping investigate an apparent crime that not only involves the Jepson wheat ranch, but the death of your former husband."

Rocky then said, "A couple of days ago, a bunch of us, including Lem, Larry, and Larry's job contractor were out here and found Joe's skeleton."

"Well, I *saw* you all down there, but I didn't know what all the commotion was about. Now Roscoe is being questioned, and Larry is gone. Lem told me he had arrested Larry, but none of this makes any sense at all."

"Well it didn't make any sense to accuse Larry, that's for sure. He's about as guilty as I am," Jenny said.

A long pause followed, so Jenny continued. "We came up here to find out what was going on, and you don't know any more than we do. Maybe we should all move on."

"My husband and son are now in the hands of the police. Maybe I'm next. This is small-town bullshit. It reminds me of my early life in Hungary. The cops don't know what they're doing and here I am surrounded by a bunch of amateur crime solvers. What's the matter with you people? Don't you have anything to do. I know the saying is anything *better* to do, but *anything* would be better than what you're doing now. Now leave me alone so I can get down to the police station and talk some sense into that idiot who's taken every member of my family into custody. His thinking seems to be, arrest everybody in Dufur, and you can be certain that one of em did it. Now get the hell out of here. All of you. And leave me alone."

Only one of the remaining four thought that Margo had made a good point, and that was Rocky. *What the hell* are *we doing?*

Jenny had no doubts. She was determined to earn that tattoo. She was going to be a criminology major with one notch already in her gun.

When Warren escorted Roscoe into the conference room Roscoe was red as a hot poker. Warren pulled out a chair for Roscoe and asked him if he wanted a cup of coffee or a soda.

"Why am I here?" Roscoe almost shouted.

"In due time, Fat-head," Lem said. "Warren, will you go back and release the prisoner we've been holding?"

"Sure thing, Lem."

When Warren exited the room, Roscoe shouted,"You must know me. I'm Ross Jepson. This isn't right."

"Relax. Jepson. The reason I brought you down here is so that you could tell me about that project of yours out at Larry's place."

"It's my place, too. I live there."

"Do you want to tell me about what you're working on out there?"

"No, it's none of your business."

"Do you really think that?"

"Of course I do. I got permits."

"I know. I signed em. I was out there to see the project a few days ago, and it looked like there was some stuff there that was different than that permit I looked at."

"I made some insignificant changes. I did not want to go through the whole permit procedure again."

"I don't remember that there was a skeleton in the permit I reviewed. Was that one of your changes?"

"I don't know anything about a skeleton."

"Did you know that hundreds of salmon swam up your so-called effluent flume?"

Warren entered the room and told Lem that their prisoner had been released. "Sit down here a minute, Warren. The guy sitting there across the table from us built a flume – or he had one built using Larry Jepson's money, I expect. And then two really strange things happened. First, most of the salmon that were migrating up the Columbia River decided to turn right at the Deschutes and go up this guy's flume instead of staying in the river. And second, when we discovered what was happening, we started taking the flume apart and found a skeleton. It turns out that the skeleton is very likely his father's. Now what do you think we ought to do with this boy?"

"I'd recommend to him that he get himself a lawyer."

"Have you got a lawyer, Roscoe?"

"No. I don't need one."

"I'm placing you under arrest for murder and poaching. You might want to consider changing your mind." Then to Warren, "Warren, will you kindly put this feller into our cell back there? After you do that, give Mrs. Jepson a call and tell her Roscoe is under arrest."

༄

Jenny and Grace entered the station a couple of hours after Roscoe was arrested. "Lem, we've got a brilliant idea," Jenny blurted."

"What's the plan, Ladies?"

"Well, we grabbed a sample of what was dripping into the settling pond. All we have to do is run it through a spectrometer and we'll know what it is. We're experts in spetrometry."

"I doubt you'd find one a them in The Dalles."

"We'll go to Portland. All you have to do is set it up with one of the universities there."

A couple of phone calls later, Lem wrote out some instructions and the two women were on their way to Portland State University.

༄

When the phone rang at the station, it was picked up by the desk clerk. "Lem, please," Jenny said.

"Who's calling?"

Jenny remembered the woman she was dealing with. This is the 9-1-1 operator, I have an emergency to report."

It worked and Jenny said to Lem, "It's perfume. We can't tell what brand, but it's perfume. Can you imagine. Roscoe

235

somehow imprinted those fish with perfume, and they came back to it."

"Thanks, Jenny. That probably explains why I saw Roscoe coming out of the Gucci Store last month. I'll go over there and see if they remember selling any perfume to him."

Lem looked out of place in the Gucci store and knew it. He guessed that Roscoe also would have looked out of place, especially in the incognito disguise he had on. Lem figured that might help the clerk remember him.

"How may I help you, sir?"

Lem showed the woman a police ID and a picture of Roscoe. "Did this guy buy anything here in the last month?"

"Yes, he did. He bought four bottles of our perfume. He did not look like someone who would buy one bottle, so it was quite a surprise when he bought four."

"Thanks, ma'am." Lem looked back from the door as he was leaving. "How much do you get for those."

"The young man bought the three ounce size for $109.99 each. I could let you have it for a little less. We have a special coming on next week."

CHAPTER FORTY-SEVEN

The visitor's room in The Dalles jail has a sign advising that conversations between prisoners and visitors may be recorded. Either Roscoe did not see it, did not believe it, or did not think it would actually be done.

When Jenny and Grace returned from Portland, Lem invited them to join him in the conference room to listen to a conversation between Roscoe and Margo that had occurred while they were in Portland. First, Lem told them of the discovery that perfume had been used as the attractant, and added that the fact that Roscoe had bought some only ten days previously, strongly suggested that Roscoe was guilty of poaching. Lem also told them that he had called the local warden to handle that part of the case. He continued, "The visit between Margo Jepson and Roscoe might surprise you." He played back the conversation.

Margo, in an angry tone: "Roscoe, did you kill your father?"

"Me? No, Mother, I thought you did."

"You thought *I* did? *I* did? He was my husband. He was gone a lot, but he was my husband. Everybody loved Joey, including me."

"I didn't know that. In fact I thought you didn't like him. I didn't, you know."

"Well for goodness sake I hope you didn't kill him."

"I told you I didn't. If I had killed him how could I possibly think you did? That's stupid, Mother."

"If you didn't kill him, then who did?"

"I could ask you the same question. How should I know?"

"Well, I'm not dumb, Roscoe. This whole wild rice scheme you've been putting us through is nonsense. Then they find the bones under the flume you built. You had to be the one who put them there, because they say they weren't there before they built the flume."

"All right, I did put the skeleton there. But I didn't kill him."

"How did you know where the skeleton was if you didn't put it there?"

"When I moved into my cabin, I could tell that the floor had been torn up, so I got curious and pried up the boards. That's when I noticed that there was a body under the floor. A body. Can you imagine that? It was a body, and it was Dad. It was eerie, Mother. He was on his back, like he was watching me, but his eyes were gone."

"And you just left him there?"

"Yes, Mother. I thought you had put him there."

"I've never even seen that place where you stay."

"I still thought that it had to be you. Who else would kill Joe Toth and put him there?"

"I can't think of anyone. You know, Roscoe, the cops are going to think that one or the other of us did it. They'll probably think it was you. Although, let's see…you were only fifteen when he disappeared. That's a little young for murder, but not out of line with the history of patricide, I expect."

"Mother, can't you see what I was trying to do?"

"No."

"I was trying to protect you."

"Protect me? I don't get it."

"Well, when I found my father under the floor of my cabin, naturally I thought it must have been you who put him there. I have to confess that I was happy to make the discovery because it meant that I would receive more of your attention. So all the time I was in college, and while I was working in the jobs I had afterwards, I was working on this plan that would divert suspicion away from you."

"Roscoe, what you should have done was leave him there. How he got there, I don't know. But during the first year after he disappeared they looked all over the place for him and never found him. They had dogs and everything. Then they gave up. They have not even thought about Joe for five years or so."

"Well, there are two things. One, it was creepy having his bones under my house. It felt like he was still looking at me. And, two, I thought it would be good to have the remains found and for Larry to get convicted. Then you and I would've had that whole ranch to ourselves. We could have raised goats and geese. Stuff like that. Maybe pigeons."

"Roscoe, you got good grades, but if you think we could make more out of goats and geese than we do with wheat, you're about as smart as that skeleton you found."

"My plan was brilliant, Mother."

"Did it work?"

"Apparently not, but I can't figure out why."

"I'll tell you why. Because it wasn't brilliant, that's why."

"But wait, Mother. Apart from all of that, I was trying to protect you. Remember, I thought you had killed my father. I had your back, Mother."

"One of the marvelous things about this situation is that you cooked up a plan that was an utter failure, and you still are trying to convince me that it was brilliant."

"It was, Mother. It was a brilliant plan. How many people could devise such a complex scheme?"

"Let's see. The outcome is that you are in jail, suspected of murder, and before you implemented the plan you had a good job working at a very promising bug plant. Apparently, your definition of brilliant is different than mine. What did they teach you down there at Berkeley U. or whatever they call it?

Did they teach you that old W.C. Fields quote, 'If you can't dazzle em with brilliance, baffle em with bullshit'?"

"Don't be so hard on me, Mother. I was trying to help you. Doesn't that count for something?"

"Yes it does, son. It counts in the evaluation of your effectiveness, which is zero – zee-row. It confirms that you are about as bright as those geese that you think we should be raising. Larry spent a million bucks on this incredibly idiotic scheme of yours, you're in jail, and will be for quite awhile, it looks like, and now we have to tear down the flume and figure out what to do with the building. You know something, Roscoe? Your father was a schemer, but he kept the stakes low, and almost everybody loved him. Somebody didn't, or he'd still be alive. But he was reasonably in touch with the real world. Try as I might, I can not figure out how any sane person could contrive anything as stupid as what you have done and present it as brilliant. Good luck, Ross. The way I see your future, you will need a lot of it."

There was a long pause in the recording – some fifteen seconds or so – with only a barely audible sound.. Suddenly, Grace said, "That's Roscoe crying. I heard him do that once before. That's him crying."

ৎৣ

Lem asked Jenny and Grace to come back the following morning to brief the warden about their analysis of the salmon attractant. They thanked Lem and headed back to their hotel. Lem then put together another news release which he faxed over to the four television networks.

"Roscoe Toth, aka Ross Jepson, is in custody at The Dalles jail under suspicion of murdering of his father, Giuseppe Toth. The senior Toth's remains were found on the Jepson wheat ranch, hidden beneath a flume that had received approval through the U.S. Army Corpse of En-

gineers permit process. No further details are available at this time."

CHAPTER FORTY-EIGHT

The television set in The Souls' clubhouse was always on, although it was rare that anyone watched it. But when Giuseppe Toth's name was mentioned, a couple of the members drifted over to see what was being said.

At the end of the short item, Boss Reynolds passed his sprinkler perc to Moose Wolcott. "What do you think?"

"Joe was a good dude."

"I figured he'd turn up dead somewhere."

"Funny guy. Whoever knocked him off was an asshole."

"He used to ride that Harley Fatboy. I wonder what ever happened to the bike."

"His old lady sold it, I think."

"Figures. I think that bitch did him."

"Doubt it. Too docile."

"Docile. Good word, Moose. I still think she had it in her."

Pork Desmond joined the conversation. "No, Margo was sweet. That little bitch had a body, too. I always used to wonder why Joe was hanging out here so much when he could go home to that."

Fuzzy Lopez came over and said, "Joey was loco, Pork. Don't try to figure out that little hoss."

Moose again, "Do you think his old lady did him?"

"Nope, Moose. In fact I know she didn't."

"You always seem to know shit like that, Fuzzy. I don't get it."

"I don't know shit *like* that. I just know *that*. I know it because of something Chance told me not too long after Joe disappeared."

ဆ

The next morning, Enrique "Fuzzy" Lopez, walked into The Dalles Police station wearing a leather jacket with "The Souls" logo on the back. "Lem around?" he asked the woman staffing the desk.

"What's it about?"

"Joe Toth."

"I'll check."

The woman called Lem on the intercom, and he emerged within a minute. "Hey Fuzz," he said.

"Yo, Lem."

"Sup?"

"Poca cosa."

"What can I do for you?"

"I know who killed Toth."

"We'd better go into the conference room."

Lem knew Fuzzy simply because they had both lived in the small town of The Dalles most of their lives. Fuzzy had had his share of minor scrapes with the law, but he was well liked by those who knew him. Lem had never known him to bully anyone. For many years Fuzz worked at The Souls' burrito stand at the Independence Day Fair. Fuzz was the last person that Lem would ever have asked anything about the disappearance of Joe Toth. "Why in the hell did you wait ten years to mention it?" Lem asked.

"For the very reason that I couldn't be absolutely sure that he was dead. No body, no murder. I guess there's the occasional murder trial with no body, but not very often, I reckon. So anyway, once I learned that his remains had been found, I knew that he had been murdered because the person who did it was a friend of a friend."

"So who do you think it was?"

"This friend told me it was Cindy Wilson."

"And who was it that told you?"

"That was a guy I knew from the club. Chance. Chance Chambers."

"How did Chance know it was Cindy?"

"Cindy was Chance's girlfriend. You remember Cindy, don't you? She owned the bar that Joe worked at. She would tend sometimes as well, but after she hired Joe, not so much."

"So why did Chance tell you?"

"Well, we were pretty good friends, and Cindy had died. You knew that she died of cancer? Some kind of brain tumor or something. So Chance just tells me. I don't know why. Like to cleanse his soul or something, maybe."

"Well if he knew about it, he was guilty of withholding evidence. That's as a minimum. Maybe even abetting."

"Well, after Cindy died, Chance disappeared. It wasn't like when Joe disappeared and nobody knew what had happened to him. Chance just took off. He told me and some other guys that he was movin' on. He had a radical bike. You could probably track it. It was a 1945 Indian – the model they made for the Army. It was cherry and ran like a dream. I always wanted that Indian. I even saved up a bunch of money and made him an offer, but he loved that cycle."

"Did Chance tell you how Cindy killed Joe?"

"He sure did. She killed him with a tire iron."

"What the hell did she do that for?"

"Cindy thought that Joe was stealing wine from her. Whether he was or not, I don't know. But he used to taunt her about it. He had a lot of leverage over Cindy even though she was the owner. Joe's night off was Monday. The receipts were always lame on Monday nights. People used to come to that bar just because Joe was there. He could sing, and tap-dance, and play the spoons, and he always had good jokes and great stories. Joe could have been in show biz, or have his own television show. He was so funny and talented.

"I think Cindy was a little jealous of his popularity. It may be that she was already getting this brain tumor, because she would get real upset about some pretty trivial shit. Anyway, Joe got off on taunting her. He was always saying things like, 'Hey, Cindy. How's your wine count today? Better check em out. I drank me a couple bottles today.' Stuff like that. Cindy would fume. One night she was at the clubhouse. Chance said it was just him and Joe and Cindy and I think one other guy. Joe had this bottle of French wine. At least he said that's what it was. He offered to give it to Cindy, but he had this smirky look on his face. She just picked up a tire iron and hit him on the head somewhere. Anyway, it killed poor Joe. So anyway, Chance knew about some old shed or cabin or something up in the woods by the Jepson place. They took poor Joe up there and put him under the floor of this place. That's what he said. I know you're going to ask me why I didn't tell anybody. Well the reason is that it was just something that I heard about. That and you got to remember we're all members of a club. We're pretty tight about watching each other's backs. The incentive to do that is that if you don't, you might wake up dead. So anyway, why am I telling you now? Cindy's dead, and Chance is long gone. I doubt you'll even pursue that guy. He moved on. That could mean he's in Mexico or Canada or Cuba – some place like that."

"I think I might have to pursue him, Fuzz. I don't think I can just write off this whole thing because you told me some story. It's hearsay, Fuzz. Not even admissible in a courtroom. Have you got any idea who the other guy was who saw this happen?"

"Nope. I don't think I ever knew. Chance just mentioned that someone else was there."

"Listen, Fuzz, chances are that it was someone in your club who's still around. It would make my job a whole lot easier if you could find out who it was. Also, it would be good to know where Chance wound up."

"Chance is gone. No one has heard from him and no one will. He could be cruisin' in Idaho, for all I know, but he'd have a different name. Chance is gone."

"That Indian ain't gone, Fuzzy."

"Now right there you could be right."

"Let me have your card, Fuzz, so I can get in touch if I need to."

Fuzz fumbled around in his leather coat and came out with a four of clubs. "Here you go, Dude. All us guys carry cards."

"Okay, let's try this. Try to find out if the other witness is still around. If you do, give me a call." Lem gave Fuzzy his card. "Now you have a card," he said.

Fuzzy Lopez left, and Lem searched a couple of data bases looking for Chance Chambers. No luck. Next, he called the department of motor vehicles and asked his contact there if she could follow a vehicle that had previously been registered in Oregon but had left the state.

"Sometimes. It depends."

"What does it depend on?"

"A lot of things. Tell me what you're looking for, Lem, and I'll check it out and let you know."

"All I've got is the make, but it's rare. It's a 1945 Indian motorcycle. It was a model built for the US Army."

"Ten-four, Lem. I'll see what I can find out. Hang on a sec." After a pause, she said, "Still there, Lem?"

"Yup, sure am, honey."

"That bike was registered to Charles Chambers. Last registration five years ago. I'll see if I can track it and call you back."

"Thanks, Molly."

୨୦

Cute redhead Molly Beck lived near Lyle, on the Washington side. She started with Oregon DMV at the age of eighteen, and now six years later was no longer a clerk, but an information specialist. She liked doing stuff for Lem, and occasionally they would have a drink together. Her drink was a martini over, which she always ordered by saying "marti-rocks" to the server. Lem was a beer man and liked Koko Brown, out of the brewery in Kona, but on draft at the bar they usually went to. Lem and Molly had a relationship, but it wasn't intense, and they both liked it that way.

Molly knew that whenever Lem asked her for an information search, it had to do with police business, which she found exciting. Consequently, she always dropped everything else to pursue Lem's requests. It took her less than an hour to find that the Indian motorcycle that Lem had asked about had not changed ownership, and now was registered in Fort Worth, Texas. She was able to verify that it was owned by Charles "Chance" Chambers, and took it one step further by looking up the motorcycle clubs in Ft. Worth. Molly found that Ft. Worth was the national headquarters for The Booze-Fighter's Motorcycle club, founded in Hollister, California, and believed to be the club portrayed in the movie, *The Wild One*, starring Marlon Brando. With this thrilling information in hand, she punched up Lem's number.

"Lem's in conference," said the officious voice that often, in the past, had caused Molly to go into a slow burn. Now she knew how to handle the little snot. "I have some information he asked me for, Troglodyte. I'll just text him and let him know you wouldn't let me pass it on."

"One minute please."

Molly repeated what she had learned and after taking it all down on a yellow pad, Lem said, "*The Wild One*," eh? That was one fine flick. Maybe we can take it in some evening soon on Netflix or something. Thanks a lot, Molly. You're special."

CHAPTER FORTY-NINE

It took Lem less than a day to get Chance Chambers on the phone. "How are things in Ft. Worth?" he asked after identifying himself.

"Couldn't be better Lem. How the hell did you find me?"

"There's a redhead over in DMV that likes to help me out with stuff like finding old Indians."

"So you found my bike and figured I still owned it?"

"Yep. Now, Chance, I heard a funny story about you. I heard this rumor, you might call it, that you were there when Joe Toth got killed. Anything to that?"

"I s'pose that could be true. True that there could be a rumor like that, I mean."

"Now for the purpose of this conversation, let's assume, just hypothetically, that Cindy Wilson dealt Toth the blow that killed him. In this hypothetical scene, what might she have used to deal that blow?"

"I don't know. When you think of all the things that a lady could use to kill a guy a lot of different things come to mind. I suppose just thinking off the top of my head that maybe something like a tire iron could do a job like that."

"Chance, I assume you know that there is a law against withholding evidence in a crime."

"Yeah, Lem. But it don't matter now, cause Cindy Wilson is dead. You can't convict a dead person of a crime, even if they committed it."

"Let's agree on that. Knowing that a dead person can't be convicted, would you be willing to swear under oath that Cindy Wilson killed Toth with a tire iron?"

"Hell no."

"Why not?"

"Man, Cindy was my girlfriend. I've never met anyone like her. Let her rest in peace. Near as I can tell, she was well thought of in Dufur. I don't want to sully her memory."

"I could have you arrested, Chance."

"I don't think so, Lem. Yeah, maybe you could, but you won't. You're too good of a guy to do some half-ass stunt like that."

"I can't comment on that officially, but in a hypothetical sense, I'd guess you're right."

ⅎ

The coroner's report noted that there was a skull fracture that would be consistent with being hit on the head with a blunt instrument. "Like a tire iron?" Lem asked the coroner.

"Yep, that could have been the weapon."

CHAPTER FIFTY

Jenny and Grace arrived at the police station after lunch. Lem had called in the morning to tell them that the warden was coming in then and wanted to talk to them. Lem was waiting and walked with them to the conference room. "I've got Roscoe in a cell back there," Lem said. "I haven't charged him with anything yet, but the charge will be poaching."

"Maybe you ought to throw murder into the charge," Jenny suggested. "That visitor's room recording makes it sound like he wasn't the murderer, but you still haven't found the perp."

"Jenny for the first time, you missed one. Don't worry, even home run hitters strike out a lot."

Jenny thought of her big hit at the cages after missing quite a few pitches. "You don't know how right you are," she said.

"Let me bring you up to date," Lem said. "Craig Campbell, the local warden, will be here in about an hour." Lem then recounted the information that he had received from Fuzzy Lopez and was confirmed by Chance Chambers .

Grace seemed relieved that her former employee was no longer a suspect in the murder. "Maybe Roscoe isn't such a bad sort after all," she said.

"He was a bad sort, all right," Lem responded. "He spent about a million dollars of his stepfather's money on a scheme that was either designed to capture fish, or else an elaborate attempt to get Larry arrested for killing Joe Toth. I'm not sure which."

Craig Campbell arrived and when Lem introduced him to Jenny, he said, "Lem tells me you have some insight or intuition about how Roscoe coaxed those Chinook up to his holding pond."

"He did it with Gucci perfume," she told him. "In fact I checked in the Gucci store and it was *Guilty Absolute Eau de Parfum*. I'm guessing that as a warden you know all about the homing instincts of salmon."

"Well, yeah. Yep. So you think he somehow imprinted the run?"

"The way I see it, he put perfume in the hatchery raceways just before the smolts were released. Have you been out to the Jepson place?"

"Yes, I have. That is one of the most bizarre scenes I've ever seen in my life. You'd have to be flat out nuts to do something like that. I don't know what Larry Jepson was thinking. I guess he fell for the wild rice story. And I expect you're right about the perfume. I'll try to get a confession out of the guy, but we've got a pretty strong poaching case if I can't."

Lem added, "I wish we could get him for something besides poaching."

"Given the nature of what he did," Craig said, "I think they'll give him his just deserts. I don't want to bore you, but we're not just talking about a minor assault on the epicure's kitchen. Salmon runs are already stressed by destruction of their habitat. Think about what it takes to get that fish out of the ocean and onto your plate. The dockside price of Chinook salmon is pushing five dollars a pound. That's around a hundred dollars a fish to the skipper and his crew. Let's say a boat catches a hundred salmon on a trip. That's 10,000 dollars worth. One trip for one boat. Now you have to add in the commerce of the processors who distribute to the retail stores and restaurants, and of course the final retail sale. You have boat builders, dry docks, engine repair shops. Plus all the equipment that outfits these commercial boats. You have fishing harbors and all the commerce around them. And right now I'm only talking about the commercial side. Sport fishing for salmon is a huge economy if you consider travel, food and lodging, boats, equipment, rentals, guide services, etc., etc., etc. Pacific Salmon annually contribute many, many millions of dollars to the economy. And it ain't just here in the Columbia River. It's up and down the entire coast from California to Alaska.

"In addition to the commercial and sport fisheries there are tribal rights to salmon that ensure that American Indians can continue to take salmon for subsistence and traditional ceremonies.

"Too many people think resource management is only for the so-called green left. They simply do not know the economic value of the industry.

"The instinctive return to their natal spawning grounds is what assures the survival of these remarkable fish, and this idiot diverted the entire run for his own reasons, whatever they might have been. The runs have been diminishing for years because of the economic development activities of humans. As you no doubt have heard, restoration by hatchery production has not been satisfactory. This was no prank that Roscoe was involved in, it was a multi-million dollar crime."

ℬ

Circuit Judge Desmond Shaw was the great grandson of Yakima Chief Desmond Birdsong. He enjoyed the privileges of the Yakima tribe and was an authority on Tribal Law, particularly as it pertained to the right to harvest Chinook salmon from the Columbia River. An avid fisherman, he felt animosity toward white society for the habitat destruction and other activities that had diminished the salmon runs, particularly the spring run on the Columbia.

Larry Jepson hired one of the top defense lawyers in the Hood River Valley to represent Roscoe, even as he privately wished the young man would be dealt with harshly. Charges against Toth were poaching, fraud, and tampering with evidence to divert suspicion. The attorney, Lester Scarsella, saw no hope in asking for a jury trial and told Roscoe that if he confessed the sentencing official might find reason for leniency. When it became known that the official would be Judge Shaw, Lester asked for sentencing to be conducted in a different jurisdiction. That request was denied.

Desmond Shaw sentenced Roscoe to twelve to twenty-two years in the State Penitentiary.

In The Oregonian it was reported that the upbraiding delivered by Judge Shaw was the most brutally criticizing speech ever observed by the reporter – more stern even than that delivered in a recent murder case.

At the end of the proceeding, Shaw asked if Roscoe had anything to say. "I was trying to protect my mother because I thought she had killed my father. The fish were returned to the river. I do not believe you should be so upset."

Shaw's response was, "Mr. Toth, if it were within my authority to do so, I would have recommended that your punishment be decided by the Tribal Council. Lacking that authority I have inflicted upon you the most severe sentence allowable under the laws of this state and this nation. In my humble opinion it is too light."

EPILOGUE

During the time that Rosco Toth was in prison, the following things happened.

Mike Simmons continued driving his truck, but never picked up another hitchhiker. He visits Jennifer when his route takes him near Berkeley and they occasionally sportfish for Chinook salmon outside the Golden Gate.

John Belton was elected to the House of Representatives, served one term, and then returned to farming. Kathy got married, moved to San Rafael and sees Jenny often.

Jeff was invited to play in the World Series of Poker and took third. His prize was around $85,000. He lives in Carson City and still plays the game he loves. Tillie received an athletic scholarship from the University of California, Davis, where she plays lacrosse.

The murder of Chad Biswell was never solved and now resides in a cold-case file in the Ames, Iowa police records.

Lem Russell applied for Chief of Police in Portland, was selected, but ultimately turned down the offer and stayed in The Dalles.

Larry Jepson developed his new building into a production facility for chanterelle mushrooms and set up a world-wide distribution to Zagat reviewed restaurants. He never visits Roscoe. Margo seldom leaves home except, on rare occasions, to visit Roscoe at the state penitentiary in Salem.

Grace Summers reached a merger agreement with an enormous industrial conglomerate, who paid one point six billion dollars for her development secrets. The market for her products, which are sold under the label Graceful Death, surpassed all expectations and the merger was deemed to be an extraordinary success by all. Grace is director of her division in the company.

The Sherbines' children assumed the enormous management responsibilities of their wheat and cattle operations. Rocky and Terri became authors and wrote this book under the pseudonym of William Leet.

Jennifer Lindsey continued to work for Grace until the merger was consummated. She graduated from Cal with a degree in criminology, minoring in resource management. She went on to get a law degree at Boalt Law School, and is now an FBI agent specializing in resource crimes. Grace shared some of the proceeds from the sale of her company with Jennifer, who currently lives in a two-story brown shingle Maybeck house in the Berkeley Hills overlooking the bay. She has a tattoo on her left shoulder that says, "I helped solve one." Since then she has solved many more.

Made in the USA
San Bernardino, CA
23 July 2018